Afro-Americans in New Jersey

Afro-Americans in New Jersey

A SHORT HISTORY

GILES R. WRIGHT

TRENTON
NEW JERSEY HISTORICAL COMMISSION, DEPARTMENT OF STATE

Copyright © 1988 by the New Jersey Historical Commission,
Department of State
All rights reserved
Printed in the United States of America

New Jersey Historical Commission, Department of State
4 North Broad Street, CN 305
Trenton, NJ 08625

Designed by Nancy H. Dallaire

Thomas H. Kean, Governor
Jane Burgio, Secretary of State

Library of Congress Cataloging-in-Publication Data

Wright, Giles R.
  Afro-Americans in New Jersey.

  Bibliography: p.
  1. Afro-Americans—New Jersey—History. 2. New
Jersey—Race Relations. I. Title.
E185.93.N54W75 1989 974.9′00496073 88-33021
ISBN 0-89743-075-1

Dedicated to the memory of my father
Giles R. Wright, Sr.
and mother
Mae Cora Whitten Wright

Contents

Acknowledgments	9
Afro-Americans in New Jersey	
Introduction	13
Colonial Period to 1790	18
1790–1870	25
1870–1910	45
1910–1940	54
1940–1980s	68
Appendixes	79
Suggested Readings	99

Acknowledgments

I am deeply indebted to several Commission staff members for their assistance in the preparation of this publication. Howard L. Green, Bernard Bush and Lee R. Parks all read various drafts of the manuscript. I also benefited from suggestions made by David S. Cohen. Evelyn Taylor ably typed all of the drafts of the manuscript. Nancy H. Dallaire deserves thanks for the design and production of the publication.

Afro-Americans in New Jersey

Afro-Americans in New Jersey

Introduction

The long Afro-American presence in New Jersey has had a paradoxical and bittersweet quality. Some observers believe that New Jersey has had the worst race relations of the northeastern states. Still, over the years the state has served as a major area of settlement for southern blacks, offering a kind of refuge or "Balm in Gilead," to cite the old Negro spiritual. Viewed through the prism of the Afro-American experience, New Jersey offers contrasting images: a place of hostility and hardship necessitating struggle, and yet a place of succor and opportunity permitting achievement.

In its treatment of Afro-Americans, New Jersey has often been likened to the South. In 1823, for example, a traveler from Connecticut passing through New Jersey expressed a common northern view and called New Jersey "the land of slavery." Twenty-six years later Dr. John S. Rock of Salem, a leading black New Jerseyan, also linked the state with the South. When it was proposed to the legislature that New Jersey secede from the Union because the Union included the slave-holding southern states, he considered the idea hypocritical because slavery still existed in New Jersey. The state, he said, "has never treated us as men.... She has always been an ardent supporter of the 'peculiar institution' [slavery]—the watchdog for the Southern plantations; and unless she shows her faith by her works, we will not believe in her."

E. Frederic Morrow, a black who was born in Hackensack in 1909 and rose to become an executive assistant to President Dwight D. Eisenhower, titled his autobiography, published in 1973, *Way Down South Up North* to characterize the experience of growing up in the state. Southern blacks who came to New Jersey during the Great Migration that was prompted by World War I—the first massive movement of blacks to the North—began referring to the state during the 1930s as the "Georgia of the North." Marion Thompson Wright, a pioneer in New Jersey Afro-American historiography, drew a similar parallel in 1943: "New Jersey is a state in which are found, so far as Negroes are concerned, practices that many people believe to exist only in the southern area of the country."

Examples of antipathy toward the darker race in New Jersey are easy to find. With the possible exception of New York, New Jersey had the most severe slave code of the northern colonies. In 1704, for example, a New Jersey law prescribed forty lashes and the branding of a T on the left cheek of any slave convicted of the theft of five to forty shillings. It dictated castration for any who attempted or had sexual relations with a white woman. A century later, New Jersey was the last northern state to enact legislation abolishing slavery; a law passed in 1804 established a system of gradual emancipation. This system actually allowed slavery to continue down to the 1860s, later than in any other northern state. New Jersey's slaves were affected by the domestic slave trade that relocated bondsmen in southern lands opened for cotton cultivation beginning in the early 1800s. Some were even delivered to southern markets, especially New Orleans, as late as the 1820s. From 1852 to 1859, the legislature appropriated $1,000 annually to transport free black New Jerseyans to Africa.

During the Civil War the state legislature passed the so-called "Peace Resolutions," which disputed President Lincoln's power to free the slaves of the Confederacy. New Jersey was the only northern state that failed to ratify the Thirteenth, Fourteenth and Fifteenth Amendments. Its most prestigious educational institution, Princeton University (known as the College of New Jersey until 1898), openly discriminated against Afro-Americans in its admission practices, and between 1848 and 1945 it had no black graduates. The state had separate black public schools, especially in South Jersey, down to the 1950s. And well into the 1960s Jim Crow segregation practices governed the access of New Jersey blacks to many movie theaters, restaurants, swimming pools, and other public accommodations.

Several theories have been advanced to explain New Jersey's racial conservatism. One theory suggests that it was caused by the

INTRODUCTION

antebellum economic ties between New Jersey and the South. This theory attributes the strong pro-Southern sentiment in New Jersey during the Civil War to the market in the South for the state's industrial products. Newark, for instance, was called an "essentially southern workshop." Both planters and plantation slaves wore shoes from this city, and there were major markets in the South for its other leather products—including carriages, saddles, and harnesses—and its clothing.

According to a second theory, the state's racial demography has primarily determined its race relations. This theory suggests that the level of Negrophobia rises with the size of the black population. The theory notes that while a large black presence does not automatically cause racist thinking, it exacerbates any existing anxiety about blacks. Those who advance this theory argue that New Jersey has generally had a larger proportion of blacks than other northeastern states. Indeed, they point out, the number and proportion of colonial New Jersey's slaves were second only to New York's, and from 1790 to 1960 New Jersey had the highest percentage of blacks of all northeastern states (see Table 1).

Third, New Jersey's type of urbanization—the "provincial character" of its towns and cities—has also been cited to explain its treatment of African-Americans. Supporters of this theory argue that although New Jersey has been highly urbanized for a considerable portion of its history (54 percent of its population in 1880 was adjudged urban), its urban areas have been towns and medium-sized cities. Attitudes towards the black race in such places, they point out, have traditionally been more conservative than those fashioned in huge metropolitan centers, where the dynamism, pace and cosmopolitan air have been more accommodating to the Afro-American quest for social justice.

Fourth, because New Jersey extends further south than any other northeastern state (its southern tip is well below Baltimore), some have argued that its racial practices are rooted in its geographical position. They maintain that since it is near Delaware and Maryland, its race relations need to be seen in the context of the border states.

The final theory, a variant of the geographical argument, poses a north-south division in the state's racial attitudes that is attributable to the metropolises at the state's opposite ends: New York and Philadelphia. According to this idea, New York's attitude towards the black race has affected the racial climate of North Jersey, while Philadelphia's has influenced South Jersey.

TABLE 1

BLACK POPULATION IN THE MID-ATLANTIC SINCE 1790
(PERCENTAGE OF TOTAL STATE POPULATION)

YEAR	NEW JERSEY	NEW YORK	PENNSYLVANIA
1790	7.7	7.6	2.4
1800	8.0	5.3	2.7
1810	7.6	4.2	2.9
1820	7.2	2.9	2.9
1830	6.4	2.3	2.8
1840	5.8	2.1	2.8
1850	4.9	1.6	2.3
1860	3.8	1.3	2.0
1870	3.4	1.2	1.9
1880	3.4	1.3	2.0
1890	3.3	1.2	2.1
1900	3.7	1.4	2.5
1910	3.5	1.5	2.5
1920	3.7	1.9	3.3
1930	5.2	4.5	3.3
1940	5.5	4.2	4.7
1950	6.6	6.2	6.1
1960	8.5	8.4	7.5
1970	10.7	11.9	8.6
1980	12.6	13.7	8.8

The arguments based on urbanization and geographical divisions appear to have the greater merit. While racial intolerance has been pervasive in New Jersey since the earliest times, South Jersey generally provided black people with a less hostile milieu until the twentieth century, and then the situation reversed. This pattern refutes the linking of any large concentration of blacks to an increase in white hostility.

Several reasons explain the pattern. Colonial South Jersey and Philadelphia had large settlements of Quakers, the first organized group in this country to oppose slavery and champion the idea that freedom was a natural right. While Quakers were not free of racist and paternalistic attitudes and did not view blacks as their social equals, their influence nonetheless minimized the scale of slavery in South Jersey and gave a more benign character to black life there than in North Jersey during the eighteenth century and most of the nineteenth century.

INTRODUCTION

The Quakers' numbers and influence waned in the last decades of the nineteenth century. South Jersey's treatment of African-Americans began to reflect its larger geographical context, and in the twentieth century its discriminatory practices resembled those of Philadelphia and the neighboring border states, Delaware and Maryland. In Philadelphia, for example, a segregated public education system endured until the 1930s, and this was true in South Jersey as well for much of the twentieth century.

The shift in the north-south pattern was also caused by twentieth century urbanization. North Jersey, with the state's larger cities—albeit they have been of a medium size—became more amenable to the interests of Afro-Americans. A lesser degree of segregation, especially in schools, shows this, although, given the small black population in some places, the economic factor also probably deterred the building of separate schools.

Considering the difficulties blacks have faced in New Jersey, the state's role as a major place of settlement for southern blacks is a paradox. Why have so many southern blacks made New Jersey their home? During the antebellum years some of the fugitive slaves using the escape routes through New Jersey stopped here, and many of them settled in the state's all-black communities. In the present century, which has brought the greatest numbers, they have come mainly in search of better work opportunities.

New Jersey's accessibility has also helped make it a destination for black migrants from the south. In all periods the state could be reached easily by the common modes of transportation—boat, train, bus and automobile. Also, occupying a strategic location between New York City and Philadelphia, huge metropolitan centers that attracted many migrants, the state was in the path of a major stream of black migration. Most of New Jersey's larger municipalities were near one of these cities and received some of their spillover. Moreover, many southern blacks evidently preferred the smaller, more manageable size of New Jersey's urban centers, which offered a slower, less hectic existence closer to that of the South.

The numbers of southern blacks moving to New Jersey account for most of the increases in the state's black population, with far-reaching historical implications. The settlement patterns of migrants have helped determine the present-day distribution of New Jersey Afro-Americans. Their points of origin, mainly along the Atlantic Coast—Delaware, Maryland, Virginia, the Carolinas, Georgia and Florida—have marked New Jersey Afro-American cultural life. Traditional folkways, beliefs and customs have been transplanted. Participants in the Great Migration, for example, have noted that a broad range of southern foods (for instance, collard greens, yams, and mullet fish) were not available in black neighborhood markets at the time of their arrival but eventually appeared because of their presence. They have also mentioned their continued use of traditional cures ("home remedies") in treating injuries and illnesses. And in 1941, when the folklorist Herbert Halpert studied the Pinelands, he collected folklore including Br'er Rabbit stories from migrants living in South Toms River. These tales, he said, represented a "living tradition that has recently been brought into South Jersey."

There were five southern black movements to New Jersey after the colonial period. Before the Civil War the migrants were free blacks and runaway slaves. Between the Civil War and World War I a larger number of Afro-Americans arrived. World War I set in motion the Great Migration; 1.5 million blacks uprooted themselves before 1930 and many came to New Jersey. World War II set off another sizable movement northward, and New Jersey again received an appreciable number of newcomers. The last major period of black southern movement to the north occurred between 1945 and roughly 1970, and again many migrants came to New Jersey.

The following pages contain a brief account of the long Afro-American past in New Jersey, from the colonial era to the 1980s. It is impossible to include every phase of this past, but it is hoped the account will present its main features and reveal the uniqueness of Afro-American life in New Jersey over the years, as well as the major circumstances that have shaped this life.

Colonial Period to 1790

It is not clear when blacks first appeared on New Jersey soil. Probably the Dutch—who were among the foremost slave traffickers of the seventeenth century—were responsible. One can speculate that Fort Nassau, erected by the Dutch West India Company in 1623 near present-day Gloucester City and occupied intermittently until 1651, probably had slaves, since the Dutch customarily used slave labor to fortify posts of this kind. Recent scholarship suggests that the few slaves in the colony of New Netherland were all in its capital, New Amsterdam (present-day Manhattan). Still, one can speculate that slaves may have been used on the scattered farmsteads of Pavonia,

COLONIAL PERIOD TO 1790

New Jersey's first permanent European settlement, which existed between 1630 and 1655 in parts of what is now Jersey City and Hoboken.

The Dutch led in introducing slaves in large numbers after the English took control of the region in 1664 and established a proprietary regime in New Jersey under John, Lord Berkeley, and Sir George Carteret. Indeed, many Dutch farmers, swearing allegiance to the new government, moved to New Jersey with their slaves. Most of these settled in Bergen, Middlesex and northern Monmouth counties.

Under the proprietary regime, which lasted until 1702, black enslavement was encouraged by law. The proprietors' *Concessions and Agreement* offered an additional sixty acres of land for every slave imported during 1664, forty-five acres for each slave imported the following year, and thirty acres for each one brought in during 1666. These inducements helped spawn a rapid increase in the slave labor force, and by 1680 slavery was well established in New Jersey.

In 1676 the colony was divided into two provinces. East Jersey, lying northeast of a straight line that ran from Little Egg Harbor to the northwest corner of New Jersey, contained the counties of Bergen, Essex, Middlesex and Monmouth. West Jersey, situated southwest of this line, consisted of Burlington, Gloucester, Salem and Cape May counties. (See Map 1.) East Jersey had the greater number of bondsmen, about 120 in 1680 out of a total population of roughly five thousand. It also enacted most of the slave laws of the proprietary period. Such laws established and protected the rights of slave ownership, provided for the maintenance of slaves, prohibited the sale of strong drink to blacks and Indians, imposed restrictions on the handling of guns by slaves, and set up a legal system adjudicating crimes committed by blacks.

After the two Jerseys became a united royal province in 1702, harsher penalties were enacted for slave infractions. In addition, the slave trade, which had continued through the proprietary period, received strong official support and became one of New Jersey's preferred branches of commerce. Since the trade was a royal monopoly and a lucrative source of revenue, this support came mainly from the crown. Queen Anne (1702–1714) urged Lord Cornbury, the first governor of the royal colony, to promote the importation of slaves "so that the colony might have a constant and sufficient supply of merchantable Negroes at moderate rates in money or commodities."

The colonial legislature hoped to meet the colony's labor needs by encouraging the importation of white servants, who were deemed

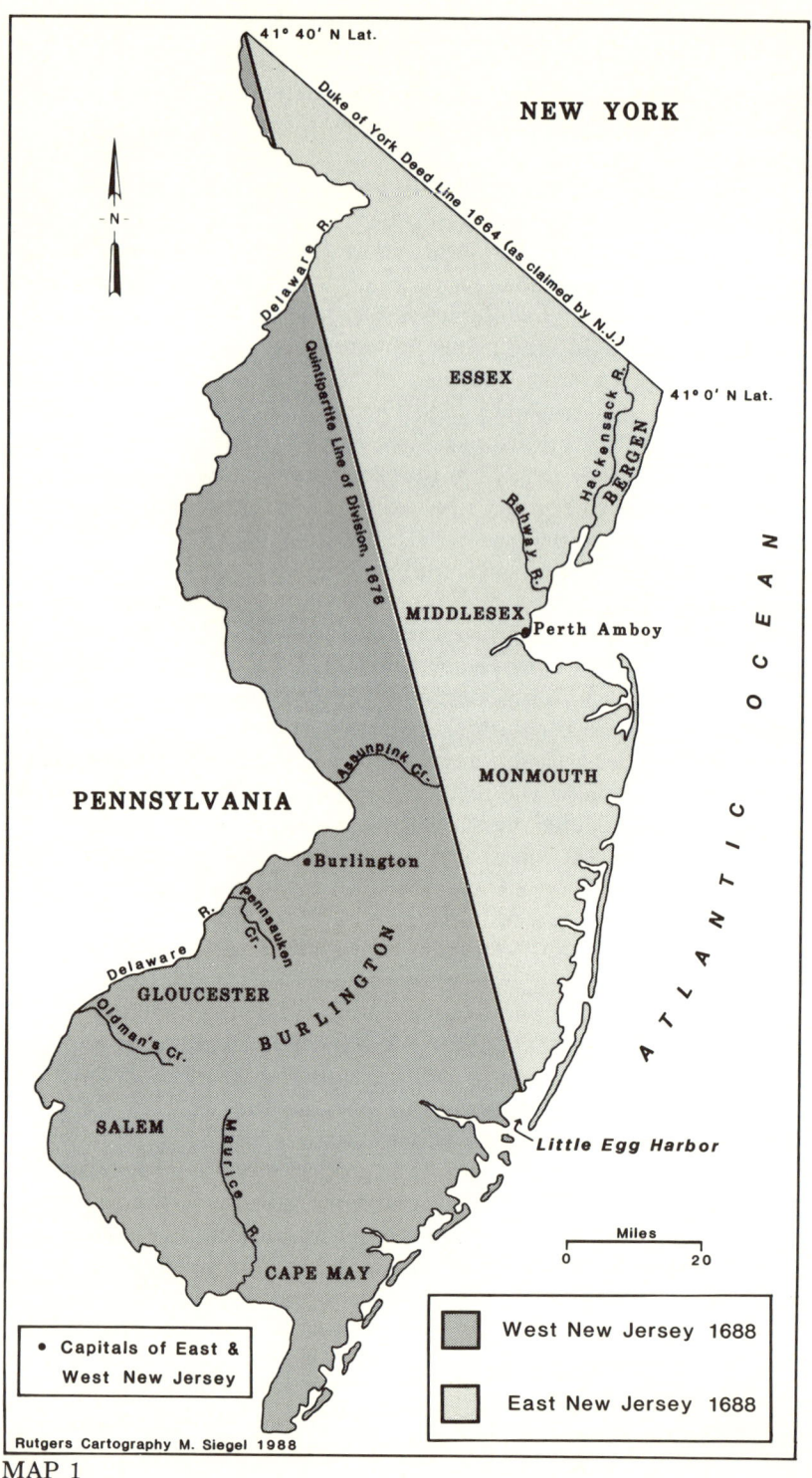

MAP 1

more assimilable. As a result it generally sought to restrict the slave trade. The crown usually prevailed, however, and between 1721 and 1769 New Jersey allowed the duty-free importation of slaves. The colony even became a haven for smugglers running slaves into neighboring New York and Pennsylvania, where tariffs on slaves were in effect. It is not surprising that the black population grew rapidly in the eighteenth century. New Jersey blacks numbered nearly five thousand by 1745 and over fourteen thousand by 1790 (see Table 2).

New Jersey's black work force, located mainly in the countryside, made a vital contribution to the colony's economic development and was remarkably diverse. Male slaves, who outnumbered females throughout the colonial period, worked chiefly in agriculture, many tending stock and raising crops for export to the West Indies. They also labored in mining, lumbering, nautical pursuits, and domestic service. Some were even skilled craftsmen: blacksmiths, millers, carpenters, shoemakers, coopers, millwrights and tanners. Most slave women were domestic servants—nannies, cooks, maids, washerwomen—or farmhands.

New Jersey slaves frequently resisted their bondage. Some ran away. Others worked slowly, destroyed tools, animals, crops and other property, and sometimes physically harmed their masters. Individual acts of vengeance, as well as slave plots both real and imagined, contributed to a widespread white fear that was expressed in severe forms of punishment designed to crush slave resistance. As early as 1695 two blacks were hanged and another was burned alive for conspiracy and the murder of a prominent Monmouth County

TABLE 2

BLACKS IN THE POPULATION OF NEW JERSEY, EIGHTEENTH CENTURY

YEAR	TOTAL POPULATION	BLACKS Number	BLACKS Percentage
1726	32,442	2,581	8.0
1738	46,676	3,981	8.5
1745	61,383	4,606	7.5
1790	184,139	14,185	7.7

slaveholder. The discovery of a slave plot near Somerville in 1734 led to the arrest of several hundred bondsmen. Two were hanged, another had an ear cut off, and many others were flogged. And in the wake of the hysteria triggered by the New York slave conspiracy of 1741, three New Jersey blacks were burned alive after being convicted of setting fire to seven barns in Hackensack.

Little is known about the precise African origins of the slaves brought into New Jersey. It appears, however, that before 1750 relatively few were imported directly from Africa. New Jersey had too little slavery to absorb full shiploads of African slaves easily. In addition, slaves newly arrived from Africa were often thought by slaveowners to be dangerous and difficult to control. New Jersey therefore tended to import bondsmen from the West Indies, especially Jamaica and Barbados; Barbadian planters even settled in New Jersey with their human property during the proprietary period. Because West Indian slaves were familiar with Western customs and work habits, they were highly prized in New Jersey, where master and slaves usually worked and lived in close proximity. After 1750 increasing numbers of slaves were shipped to North America directly from Africa. At the same time, their overall importation into New Jersey declined after that year, and by the time of the War of Independence it had virtually ceased.

Those slaves that did come to the colony fresh from Africa probably contributed to the retention of African culture in New Jersey during the slave era. Certainly an African style marked the way some danced, sang, played instruments, and paraded. Well into the early 1800s New Jersey slaves did the "shingle dance" in holiday festivities at the Catharine Market in New York City. The rhythms of this dance were said to resemble those of the ring shout, an African-influenced circle-dance style seen in southern black churches as late as the mid-twentieth century.

In 1786 New Jersey reached a milestone in the struggle against slavery by outlawing its slave trade. The fear of slave rebellions may have encouraged this development, many whites believing their security would be jeopardized by adding fresh African slaves to a black population already menacingly large. Another influence was the crusading work of early foes of slavery like John Woolman, a Quaker from Mount Holly, whose writings sparked efforts to eliminate slaveholding among his coreligionists. As a young man in 1743 he first voiced his opposition to black bondage. By 1775, three years after his death, the antislavery sentiments he represented were being promoted among non-Quakers as well. In that year a group of Quakers from Chesterfield submitted the first petition ever to the legislature for an abolition law. Three years later, William Livingston, New Jersey's first state governor, also asked the assembly to require the manumission of slaves.

Throughout New Jersey's early history its black population was unevenly distributed. During much of the slavery period about 75 percent of the bondsmen were found in the counties of Bergen, Essex, Middlesex, Hunterdon, Somerset, and Monmouth (see Map 2). These counties tended to be more economically developed and to have labor scarcities. They also had more Dutch, German, and non-Quaker settlers. Perth Amboy was the principal slave entry port for these counties. Along with New York and Philadelphia, it was a leading slave port for the Middle Colonies. Cooper's Ferry (now Camden) was its counterpart in the southern counties that had mainly constituted West Jersey. Largely because of the opposition of Quakers and because the region had a more sufficient number of white settlers than East Jersey, slavery was much less extensive here.

A north-south dichotomy also developed in the distribution of the free black population, which appeared as early as the 1680s. The Quaker-settled counties of South Jersey tended to have the highest absolute and relative numbers of freedmen, while North Jersey counties, especially Bergen and Somerset, contained the smallest.

In 1790 roughly 20 percent of New Jersey's 14,185 blacks were free. The Revolutionary War helped liberate many New Jersey slaves. Some took advantage of its chaos and fled their masters. Others joined the New Jersey militia or Continental army and were manumitted. Still others served with the British, spurred by the "Emancipation Proclamation" issued by Virginia's royal governor, Lord Dunmore, in 1775, which promised freedom to any slave who fought for the crown; some of these departed with the British at the war's conclusion. And occasionally owners set their slaves free, in accordance with the ideals advanced to justify the war. For example, Moses Bloomfield of Woodbridge, whose son Joseph later served as the state's fourth governor, freed his fourteen slaves on July 4, 1783, at a public ceremony. Pointing to them, he said:

> As a nation we are free and independent—all men are created equal—and why should these, my fellow citizens, my equals, be held in bondage? From this day they are emancipated, and I hereby declare them free and absolve them of all servitude to me, or my posterity.

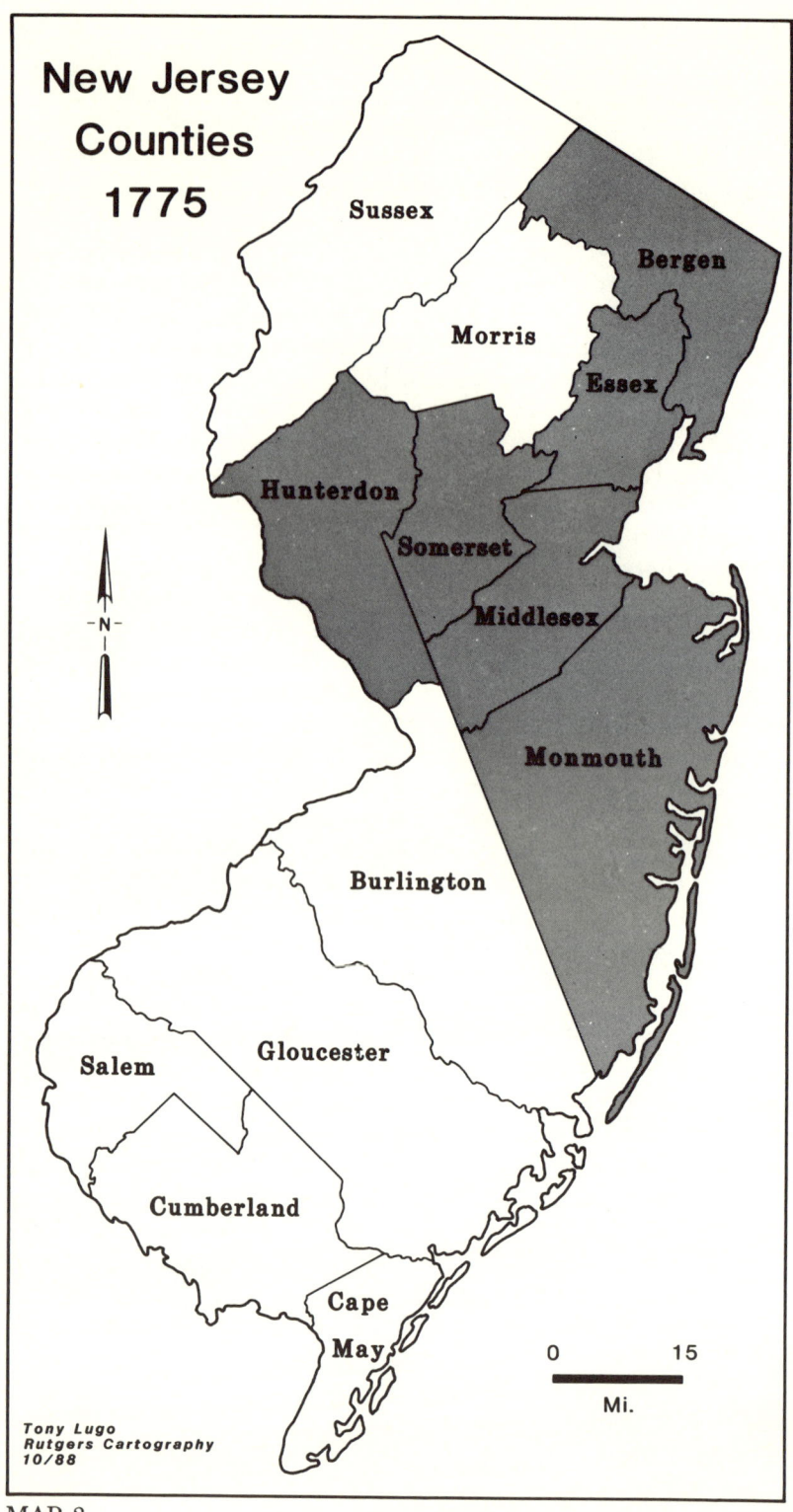

MAP 2

1790–1870

During the eighty years following the establishment of the federal government in 1789, black New Jersey life underwent momentous changes. The greatest was the end of slavery. New Jersey's slave population reached its absolute peak of 12,422 in 1800 (distributed in a manner similar to its distribution in 1810—see Map 3). Four years later legislation was passed to abolish slavery gradually. It reflected a succession of laws, starting with the abolition of the slave trade in 1786, that one historian believes constituted a "well thought out program leading to abolition." This "program" even aimed to prepare blacks to accept the responsibilities of freedom. Among the laws associated with it were one prohibiting slave abuse, one liberalizing manumission requirements, and one requiring slaveholders to teach their slaves under twenty-one to read.

Under the 1804 act, all children born of slaves after July 4, 1804, were to be freed after serving as apprentices to their mothers' masters—females after twenty-one years, males after twenty-five. The New Jersey Society for Promoting the Abolition of Slavery, which existed from 1793 to 1812, helped bring about this legislation. The society advocated the gradual elimination of slavery; its president stated in 1804 that it was not "to be wished, much less expected, that sudden and general emancipation would take place." The society realized that this moderate stance had a greater chance of success than a more radical plea for immediate and total abolition.

Some historians also attribute the passage of the 1804 act in part to a provision that benefited slavemasters. This was the abandonment clause, a thinly veiled scheme to compensate the owners for abolition. Under its provisions a master had to maintain the children of his female slaves for one year but could then abandon them to the public overseers of the poor. Once they were declared paupers, they could be bound out to service, with the state paying their new master three dollars apiece per month for maintenance. Invariably it was the original master to whom the children were bound. The system became so costly to the state that the clause was repealed in 1811.

By 1820 the abolition law of 1804 had for the first time enabled free black New Jerseyans (12,460) to outnumber those still in bondage (7,557). Still, its gradualist approach made it the target of new protest. New Jersey's second major abolitionist organization, the New Jersey Anti-Slavery Society—formed in 1840 as an outgrowth of the

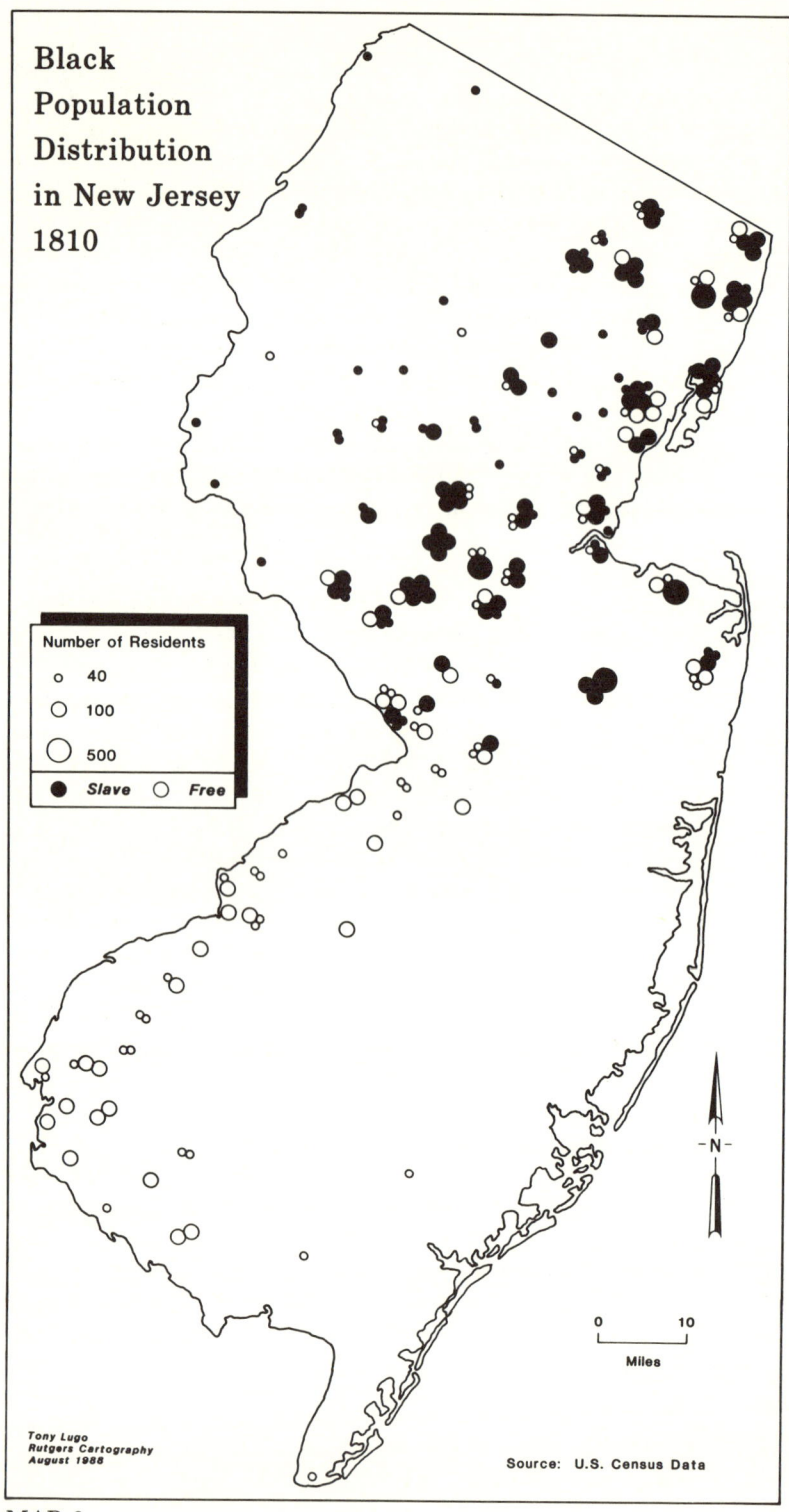

MAP 3

militant abolitionism of the 1830s—called for total and immediate emancipation. It submitted petitions to the legislature down to 1844, and then argued that the state's second constitution, adopted in that year, automatically outlawed slavery through its "Bill of Rights." The society lost this legal argument in *State* v. *Post,* which was adjudicated by the New Jersey Supreme Court in 1845. The court held that the framers of the constitution had not intended to apply their equal rights doctrine "to man in his private, individual or domestic capacity; or to define his individual rights or interfere with his domestic relations, or his individual condition." Had the framers intended to abolish slavery, the court reasoned, they "would have adopted some clear and definite provision to effect it, and not have left so important and grave a question ... to depend upon the doubtful construction of an indefinite abstract political proposition."

The society continued to petition the legislature, and in 1846 the state's second major emancipation law was passed. While this law formally outlawed slavery, it did not really emancipate all those covered by it. All black children born after its passage were declared free. But those blacks who were already slaves became "apprentices" for life. Their new status, however, afforded them greater legal protection. They could sue for their freedom if they were abused; they could not be sold without their written consent; they could not be sold out of the state. By 1860 their number had been reduced to eighteen. In 1865 the Thirteenth Amendment to the United States Constitution finally ended involuntary servitude in New Jersey.

While the 1846 apprenticeship system fell short of complete emancipation, it accomplished two objectives of its proponents. First, by obligating slaveowners to continue supporting their slaves, it prevented the slaves (of whom there were nearly seven hundred in 1846, mostly over fifty-five years of age) from becoming wards of the state. Second, it adhered to a long-standing tradition in New Jersey of respect for property rights; it abolished slavery without confiscating the property of the slaveholders.

The continued existence of slavery in New Jersey during the antebellum period suggests that there was considerable sympathy in the state for the South as its rift with the North deepened. Such sympathy was not pronounced at first. As late as 1849, for example, the state legislature, in a resolution addressed to the state's Congressional delegation, condemned the extension of slavery to any territory annexed to the United States. During the 1850s, however, the sentiment that gave rise to such resolutions decreased. The southern market for the products of New Jersey industries (such as shoes, clothing, and leather goods) expanded during this decade, and a significant part of that market involved the provisioning of slaves by their owners. White New Jerseyans increasingly felt that the abolition of southern slavery would ruin them economically. First, they feared that freed slaves would not buy their shoes and clothes from the suppliers their owners had used. Second, they believed abolition would propel hordes of emancipated bondsmen north to compete for jobs. In addition, the doctrine of states' rights was widely supported in New Jersey; many believed that the question of slavery should be decided by each state. Thus it is no surprise that New Jersey was one of the few northern states that sanctioned the Fugitive Slave Act of 1850. This law permitted runaways to be seized and returned to the South. New Jersey did not nullify it, as most other northern states did under what were popularly known as "personal liberty" laws. Underground Railroad passengers therefore had to proceed with caution in the state. New Brunswick in particular was a dangerous station, because slave hunters headquartered there to watch for fugitives crossing the bridge over the Raritan River.

By 1860 New Jersey—the only northern state that Lincoln did not carry in the presidential election that year—was divided on how best to deal with the South. Many people, mindful that the state had played an important role in the framing and ratifying of the nation's Constitution and had been the first to ratify the Bill of Rights, were devoted to preserving the Union. After the Civil War erupted on April 12, 1861, and the government made its initial request to the states for troops, New Jersey was the first to meet its obligation, supplying four regiments by May 5. By October 1862 some twenty-seven New Jersey regiments were in the field. In all, over 88,000 New Jerseyans participated in the war and 6,300 died. Among these troops were 2,872 blacks, of whom 469 died. Since the state did not organize any "colored" regiments, black New Jersey troops were assigned to other army regiments and credited to New Jersey.

At the same time, New Jersey also developed into a stronghold of support for the southern secessionists. The state's politics were heavily influenced by pro-Southern feeling during the Civil War and the Reconstruction period. Democrats gained control of the State House and the legislature in 1861. In 1863 they passed peace resolutions opposing the emancipation of the slaves and asking the federal government to appoint a peace commission to meet Southern representatives and end the war. Lincoln lost New Jersey again in 1864.

In 1865 the legislature, still controlled by the Democrats, refused to ratify the Thirteenth Amendment, which abolished slavery.

In 1866 the Republicans elected a governor and regained control of the legislature. Their legislature ratified the Fourteenth Amendment, which guaranteed the citizenship rights of everyone born in the United States. But even this legislature refused to give the franchise to the state's blacks. After the Republicans lost control in 1868 the legislature rescinded its ratification of the Fourteenth Amendment. In 1870 it rejected the Fifteenth Amendment, which extended the franchise to all races. Enough states ratified both amendments to make them the law of the land, however, and black males in New Jersey received the franchise in spite of the state's racial conservatism.

By 1870 persons of African descent in New Jersey had undergone a profound transformation in cultural form and modality, from African to Pan-African (representing the melding of different African cultures), to Afro-American. This transition had been under way in the American colonies as early as the late seventeenth century. Blacks, outnumbered by whites, increasingly native-born, and needing adaptive strategies to withstand their ordeal, began to adopt the manners and customs of their land of enslavement. This acculturative process took place differently in the three distinct slave systems of colonial America—the Chesapeake Bay, the Carolina and Georgia low country, and the nonplantation system of the North. In the North the transformation into Afro-Americans occurred relatively early—during the colonial period—and on a massive scale, and it was uniform among both rural and nonrural populations. Still, since acculturation did not mean the shedding of all vestiges of African traditions, some black New Jerseyans down to the 1870s probably remained culturally African to a degree. Since blacks in Philadelphia were continuing to dance the ring shout as late as the 1870s, it is likely that their Afro-American neighbors in New Jersey as well were keeping the tradition alive.

Facilitating the cultural metamorphosis of northern blacks was the "First Emancipation," the creation of a free black population. New Jersey's southern region in particular figured prominently in this development. It was a part of the Delaware Valley, where, due to a strong Quaker presence and influence, black slaves were first manumitted in very significant numbers.

The emergence of a free black population aided considerably the growth of black organizations and institutions of a non-African nature and character. These new institutions sought basically to promote the race's general welfare and to ameliorate the harsh conditions of black life. They included fraternal lodges, benevolent societies, literary societies and temperance organizations. The first four black fraternal lodges were organized between 1845 and 1847 in Trenton, Burlington, Camden and Salem. By the late 1860s Camden had a baseball team—the Blue Sky Club—which competed against other early black teams from Brooklyn, Philadelphia, Chicago, Washington, D.C. and Harrisburg.

Down to 1870 New Jersey Afro-Americans gave their greatest attention to the formation of churches and schools. There is evidence that black congregations existed in New Jersey as early as 1800. Salem's Mt. Pisgah Church, the only New Jersey congregation represented at the founding conference of the African Methodist Episcopal (AME) Church in Philadelphia in 1816, likely dates from that year. Its establishment can probably be attributed to the influence of Richard Allen, founder of the AME Church, who preached in South Jersey during the 1780s as an itinerant minister.

By 1818 AME churches had been established in Princeton and Trenton. Churches representing other denominations also appeared. In 1822 the Clinton Memorial Church was organized in Newark, the first AME Zion Church in New Jersey and probably the first black congregation in Newark. The Plane Street Presbyterian Church was established in Newark in 1831; its minister between 1840 and 1845 was Samuel E. Cornish, the abolitionist who had cofounded *Freedom's Journal,* the first Afro-American newspaper, in 1827. In 1832 Camden's oldest black religious institution, the Macedonia African Methodist Episcopal Church, was formed. By the time of the Civil War the black communities in New Brunswick, Red Bank, Montclair, Woodbury, Woolwich, Allentown, Fair Haven, Manalapan, Elizabeth, Rahway, Burlington and Mount Laurel had established churches. The overwhelming majority of these belonged to three denominations: AME, AME Zion, and Presbyterian.

Some of the early black churches assumed the responsibility of meeting the educational needs of the race, which sympathetic whites, especially Quakers, had started to accommodate as early as the 1780s. The AME Zion Church in Newark was in the forefront. In 1826 it began providing black youths and adults with the fundamentals of a common school education—reading, writing, spelling, and ciphering. Soon blacks in Newark started to institutionalize their educational efforts in other ways. In 1828 Abraham and John King organized what became the "Colored School," a pioneer institution that

Samuel E. Cornish (1795–1858), abolitionist, journalist and minister, became a New Jersey resident in 1838, living in Belleville. He later moved to Newark, where he became the pastor of the First Presbyterian Church on Plane Street. Convinced that the black race had a future in the United States, he was one of the most vigorous and outspoken opponents of the American Colonization Society's efforts to persuade free blacks to settle in Africa. Cornish was also among the Afro-American leaders that, beginning in the 1830s, increasingly referred to black people in the United States as "colored" rather than "African." He argued that "African" encouraged white colonizationists to believe that black people desired to return to Africa. Courtesy of the Schomburg Center for Research in Black Culture, New York Public Library.

continued to operate until 1909. James Baxter, New Jersey's foremost black educator of the nineteenth century, was principal from 1864 until its end. Black individuals and groups in New Brunswick, Princeton, Bordentown, Perth Amboy, Bridgewater, and other communities replicated the work of the Kings over the next several decades. Such efforts were complemented by those of white philanthropic and religious bodies such as the Quakers and the Episcopal Church.

Increasingly, however, public education systems developed in New Jersey, and the responsibility of educating black children was assumed by the communities they lived in. Some communities educated black children in racially mixed schools, while others established separate facilities for them. In 1829 the state began to provide some funds for education, leaving school districts to make up the difference by levying school taxes or, if they preferred, by charging tuition fees. Most cities provided free education. But some black students had to pay for their education, especially in towns and villages, until 1871, when legislation was enacted that forbade communities to charge educational fees. New Jersey was the last of the thirty-seven states then in existence to give its children free schooling; even the reconstructed southern states preceded it.

After 1790, as the ranks of freed blacks swelled, the Afro-Americans' increasing race consciousness led them to grapple with various forms of racial injustice. They focused much of their attention on southern slavery; they seem to have left it mainly to white abolitionists such as the New Jersey Anti-Slavery Society to attack the continuing slavery in New Jersey. In 1834 Newark blacks formed an auxiliary of William Lloyd Garrison's American Anti-Slavery Society; it was the state's first black abolitionist body. Black New Jerseyans also attended the various pre-Civil War meetings of the Convention Movement, a broad spectrum of northern black leaders in the forefront of political protest. From 1830 to the 1870s these conventions deliberated on ways to improve the conditions of the black race and to chart its future direction.

Perhaps the prime grievance of Afro-Americans in New Jersey down to 1870 was their disfranchisement. In 1807 the state legislature restricted voting rights to white males, eliminating privileges that the state's 1776 constitution had extended to both blacks and women. Despite immediate and sustained black opposition to the 1807 restriction, the state's 1844 constitution continued to limit the franchise to white men.

African-Americans redoubled their efforts to acquire the ballot.

James M. Baxter (1845–1909) came to Newark in 1864 from Philadelphia to serve as the principal of the Colored School. A prominent community leader, he was a staunch foe of school segregation throughout his forty-five years in this post. One of his sons later served in the New Jersey legislature, and one of his granddaughters was the first Afro-American to be admitted to the New Jersey College for Women. Courtesy of the Newark Public Library.

To that end the first statewide black convention was convened at Trenton's Zion AME Church in 1849. Delegates included some of the state's most distinguished blacks. One was Dr. John S. Rock from Salem, a physician and dentist, who later became the first black attorney to practice before the United States Supreme Court. Another, Ishmael Locke of Camden County, was a teacher who had served as the principal of the Institute for Colored Youth in Philadelphia. (His grandson, Alain Locke, became the first black Rhodes Scholar, a philosopher and "guiding spirit" of the Harlem Renaissance in the 1920s.) The pastor of the church where the convention was held was the Reverend W. T. Catto. His son, Octavius V. Catto, a Philadelphia educator and a leader of the successful battle in the 1860s to end the city's streetcar segregation, was killed in 1871 in rioting after blacks voted under the newly acquired protection of the Fifteenth Amendment.

In requesting the franchise, the convention of 1849 not only petitioned the legislature, but it also addressed a broadside to the citizens of New Jersey. The broadside adopted a particularly suppliant tone in the hope of enlisting the widespread support of white New Jerseyans:

> Therefore we now appeal to you in the face of your assertions, and in respect of your justice, your patriotism, your intelligence, your honesty and love of liberty—and in remembrance of your accountability to Him from whom cometh every good and perfect gift—requesting that you will use your influence, each for himself, in assisting us in this our purpose of obtaining for ourselves and our posterity, the blessings and perquisites of liberty in the exercise of the elective franchise, or right of suffrage; which we respectfully ask as a right belonging to us in the character of *men*; but heretofore withheld as an attache of color, or in the conservative spirit of some, and the ignorance, envy and prejudice of others.

This was followed by similar petitions and appeals from the black community. In 1865 another convention in Trenton, organized by the short-lived Equal Rights League of New Jersey, produced an appeal addressed to "the people of New Jersey." All these efforts proved ineffective. As noted earlier, only the Fifteenth Amendment in 1870 finally restored suffrage to New Jersey Afro-Americans. Thomas Peterson Mundy, one of Perth Amboy's leading black citizens, was the first Afro-American in the nation to cast a vote under this amendment. He voted in a municipal election on March 30, 1870. Within the next year, as the Reconstruction Amendments prompted other Afro-American gains in New Jersey, a black in West Milford became the first to serve on a jury in New Jersey. In 1875 the word "white" was removed from the voter qualifications in the state constitution.

The American Colonization Society (ACS), established in 1816, and its state auxiliary, the New Jersey Colonization Society, organized in 1817, were another target of black New Jerseyan protest. These organizations, convinced that free blacks could not advance in America, sought to resettle them as "civilizing agents" on the African continent. Their members included prominent New Jerseyans like Commodore Robert Field Stockton, Theodore Frelinghuysen, General John Frelinghuysen, Samuel Bayard, and the Reverend Robert Finley of Basking Ridge, a Presbyterian clergyman and a founder of ACS. In condemning them, New Jersey blacks affirmed their own commitment to a permanent residence in this country and to an identity as Afro-Americans. If they went to Africa, they argued, they would be abandoning their kith and kin who were locked in bondage. For them the Colonization Society's efforts actually masked a scheme to rid the nation of free black opponents of slavery and to deprive the race of much of its articulate and concerned leadership.

Between 1790 and 1870 important demographic changes for New Jersey Afro-Americans also occurred. For example, the growth rate of the black population declined perceptibly until 1860. Between 1820 and 1840, in particular, blacks increased in number by fewer than 2,000, from 20,017 to 21,718 (see Table 3). By contrast, during the

TABLE 3

BLACK POPULATION GROWTH IN NEW JERSEY, 1790–1870

YEAR	TOTAL	PERCENTAGE OF INCREASE
1790	14,185	—
1800	16,824	18.6
1810	18,694	11.1
1820	20,017	7.1
1830	20,557	2.7
1840	21,718	5.6
1850	24,046	10.7
1860	25,336	5.4
1870	30,658	21.0

same period New York's black population grew from 39,367 to 50,031 and Pennsylvania's from 30,413 to 47,918. A large influx of white immigrants during the antebellum period raised the white population much faster. As a result, the black proportion of the total population declined sharply, from 7.7 percent in 1790 to 3.4 percent in 1870.

North and South Jersey offer interesting contrasts in black population growth between 1790 and 1870. Although blacks in 1860 in the northern counties were concentrated in the same areas as in 1790 (see Map 4), they constituted a far smaller percentage of the region's total population by the end of the period. While the heavy influx of foreign-born whites in part explains this, a substantial emigration of free blacks is probably also involved. Between 1840 and 1860, for example, the number of free blacks in New Jersey's northern counties increased by only 1,837, from 13,646 to 15,483 (see Table 4). The region contained those areas that were traditionally most hostile to blacks. In these areas slavery endured longest, and as the immigrant population grew, white workers increasingly viewed free blacks as a threat to their occupational security. Newark was among the cities to which the ugly New York City draft riots of July 1863 spread, riots in which many

TABLE 4

BLACK POPULATION IN NORTHERN NEW JERSEY, MID-NINETEENTH CENTURY

COUNTY	1840 Free	1840 Slave	1860 Free	1860 Slave
Bergen	1529	222	1663	
Essex	1908	20	1757	
Hudson	319	11	653	
Hunterdon	778	35	800	4
Mercer	2319	22	2225	
Middlesex	1535	28	1308	1
Monmouth	2180	85	2658	
Morris	911	37	687	1
Passaic	706	96	559	2
Somerset	652	105	1597	9
Sussex	354	13	324	
Union			865	
Warren	455	8	387	1
Total	13,646	682	15,483	18

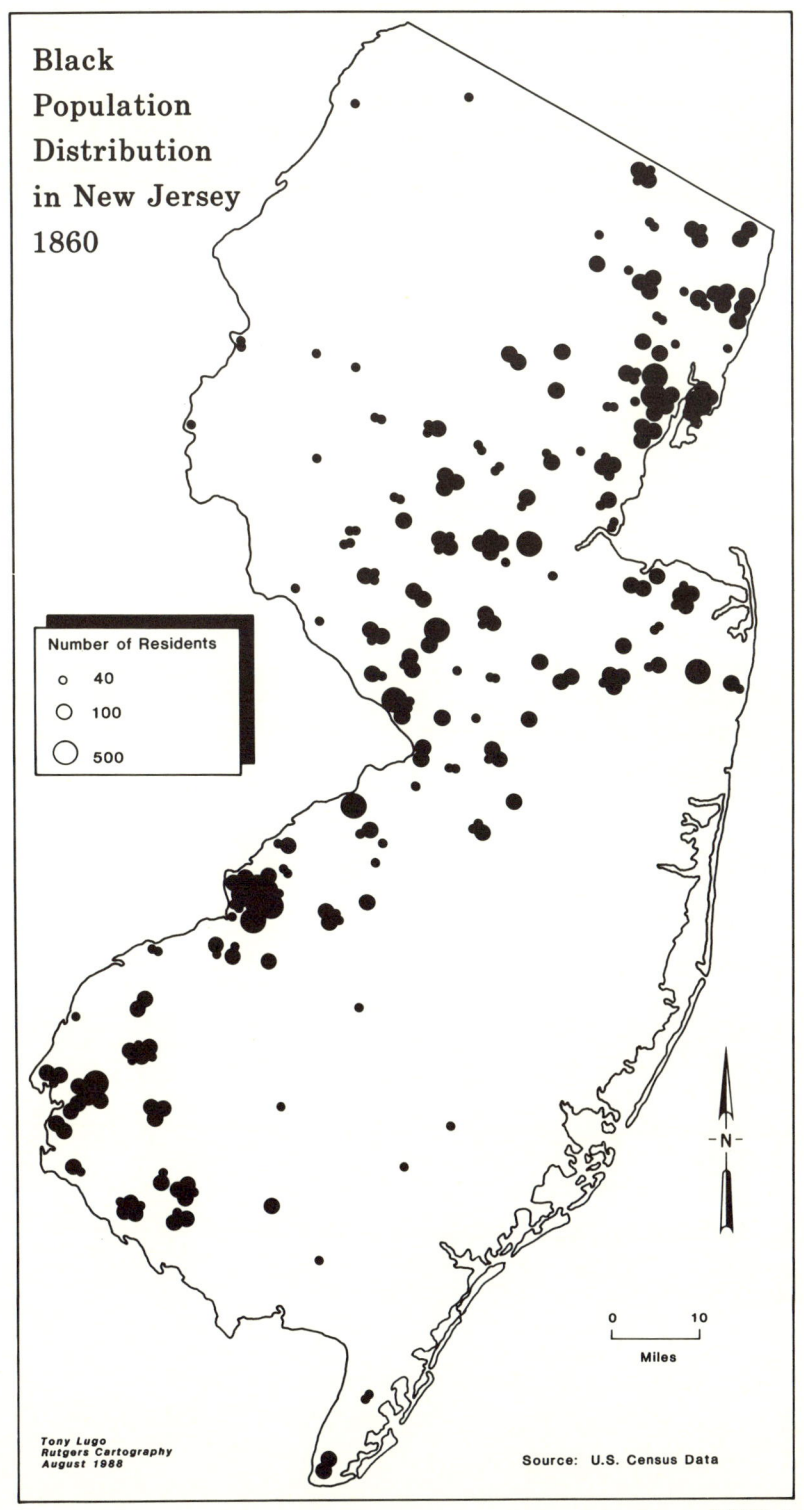

Black Population Distribution in New Jersey 1860

Number of Residents
- ○ 40
- ○ 100
- ○ 500

Tony Lugo
Rutgers Cartography
August 1988

Source: U.S. Census Data

MAP 4

white workers, perceiving abolition as the cause of the war they were being conscripted to fight in, singled out blacks as the targets for their violence.

Fear of the Fugitive Slave Law of 1850 may also explain why the number of North Jersey blacks increased so little, since the state government cooperated with southern states in returning runaway slaves. In addition, a pronounced mood to limit the number of free blacks in the state took hold before the Civil War. It was reflected in proposed legislation under which all free blacks desiring to remain in the state would have to register or risk fines and arrest as fugitives. The movement to discourage free blacks seems to have succeeded best in North Jersey.

On the other hand, the free black population in New Jersey's southern counties grew from 5,524 in 1840 to 9,853 in 1860, an increase of 4,329 (see Table 5). In 1870 Camden County had more blacks than any other county, and five southern counties—Camden, Cumberland, Salem, Burlington, and Gloucester—had over two-fifths of the state's total black population although they constituted only about one-fifth of the overall population (see Table 6). Some communities in these counties, especially Camden, Stockton, Newton, Center, Burlington, Deptford, Mannington, Pilesgrove, and Fairfield, had sizable numbers of Afro-Americans.

TABLE 5

BLACK POPULATION IN SOUTHERN NEW JERSEY, MID-NINETEENTH CENTURY

COUNTY	1840 Free	1840 Slave	1860 Free	1860 Slave
Atlantic	256		194	
Burlington	1643	1	2224	
Camden			2574	
Cape May	198		273	
Cumberland			1295	
Gloucester	1631		707	
Ocean			124	
Salem	1796		2462	
Total	5,524	1	9,853	

1790–1870

TABLE 6

BLACKS IN THE POPULATION OF FIVE
SOUTHERN NEW JERSEY COUNTIES (BURLINGTON, CAMDEN,
CUMBERLAND, GLOUCESTER AND SALEM), 1870

	NEW JERSEY POPULATION	POPULATION OF FIVE COUNTIES Number	Percentage
Total	906,096	179,999	19.9
Black	30,658	12,447	40.6

Most of the growth in South Jersey's black population down to 1870 arose from a steady arrival of southern blacks during the antebellum period. Having several Underground Railroad routes (see Map 5), the region became a haven for slaves escaping the South. Harriet Tubman, the fugitive slave from Maryland who became a fearless "conductor" of the Underground Railroad, primarily of Delaware and Maryland slaves, spent periods of time in Cape May between 1849 and 1852 working as a servant in hotels to earn money for her forays south. Leaving Cape May for the last time in the fall of 1852, she made a fifth journey into Maryland and took nine fugitives out.

Others adding to southern New Jersey's black population were free blacks from the South. The region appealed to them, for one reason, because of its Quakers, with their traditional liberal disposition towards blacks. Perhaps more important, by 1870 New Jersey had several all-black communities; in this it was unique among northern states. While some of these settlements were in North Jersey—for example, Skunk Hollow in Bergen County—most were in the southern part of the state. Notable examples were Guineatown and Saddlertown in Camden County, Timbuctoo in Burlington County, and Gouldtown in Cumberland County. Two that were particularly attractive to southern blacks were Springtown in Cumberland County and Lawnside in Camden County.

Located in the northern end of Greenwich Township, Springtown was established around 1800 by slaves who had been manumitted or who had escaped from bondage in Delaware, Maryland or states further south. Nearby Quakers sold small tracts of land to them. Samuel Ringgold Ward, the abolitionist orator known as "the black

MAP 5

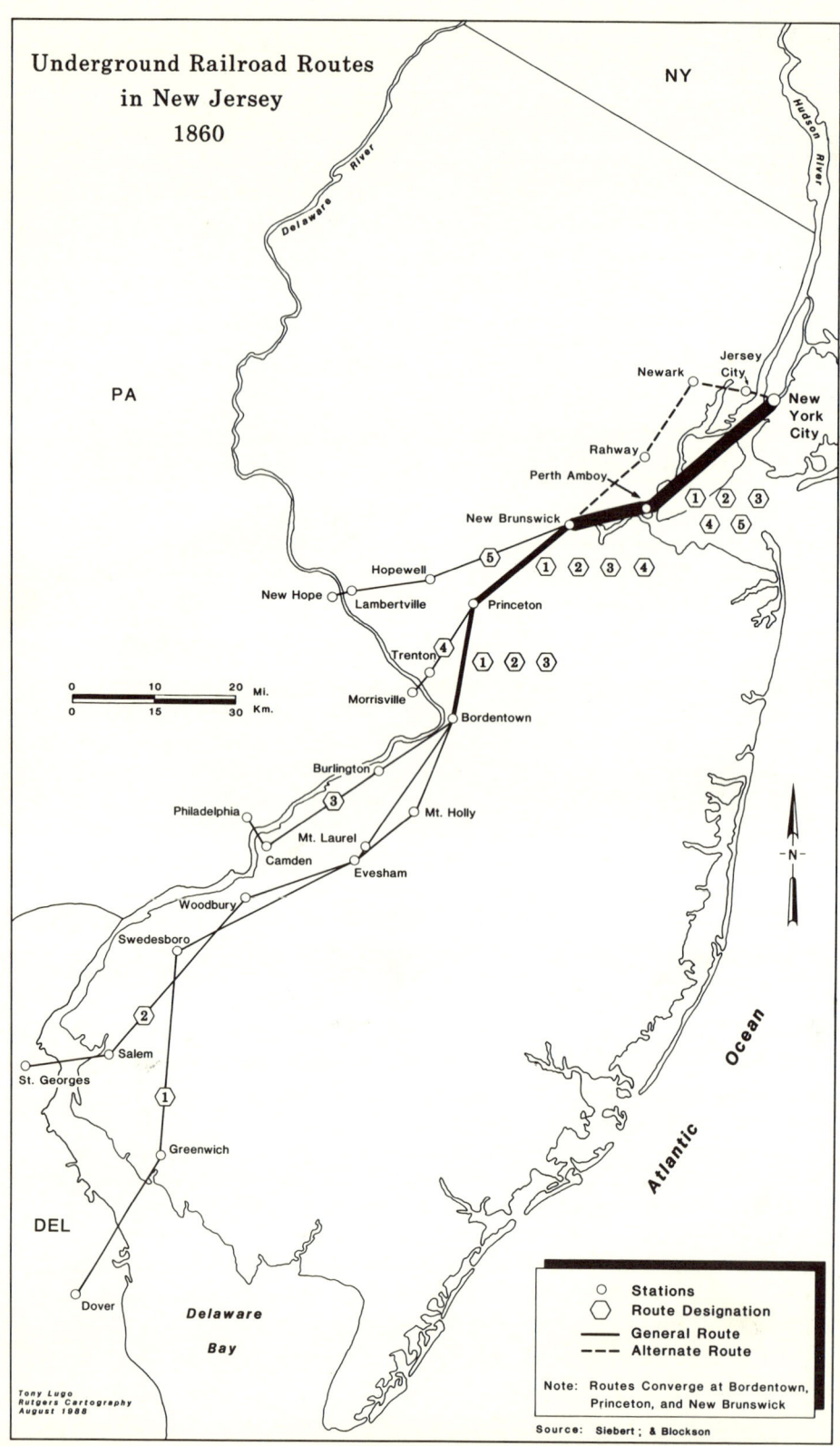

Daniel Webster," lived there from 1820 to 1826. In his autobiography he described the cooperation between local Quakers and blacks. The settlement was an important station on the Underground Railroad during the antebellum period, especially for slaves escaping from the Delmarva peninsula. Springtown reached its apogee in the 1870s, declining thereafter because many of its inhabitants moved to Camden, Philadelphia, and Wilmington. Today it has about one hundred residents.

Among Springtown's early settlers was Levin Steel, who came from the eastern shore of Maryland. Shortly after arriving he changed his surname to Still, a name associated today with one of New Jersey's outstanding black families. One of his sons was William Still, the Philadelphia abolitionist who wrote *The Underground Railroad,* an invaluable collection of documents and stories about this clandestine network. Another distinguished son was James Still, a practitioner of folk remedies in Medford, who came to be known as "The Black Doctor of the Pines." Dr. Still was one of the foremost spokesmen for the Afro-American community in New Jersey during the nineteenth century. In his autobiography, published in 1877, he outlined a course of action for the race. A leading student of New Jersey Afro-American history, Clement A. Price, has pointed out that this program bore a strong resemblance to the one set forth later in the century by Booker T. Washington, the "Sage of Tuskegee." For example, Still admonished blacks to comport themselves well, convinced that such behavior would be justly rewarded:

> My colored friends, should you conduct yourselves on true moral principles, not gaudy in manners nor boisterous in talk, your ways calm and decisive, your word so sacred that 'tis never violated, your promises fulfilled, your debts paid, modest in all things and meddlesome in none, you shall find the monster Prejudice only a thing to be talked about. Merit alone will promote you to respect.

The early history of Lawnside, about ten miles southeast of Camden, is similar to that of Springtown. It too was established in the latter part of the eighteenth century, became an Underground Railroad station, and benefited from the assistance of neighboring Quakers. It was known initially as Snowhill. The land comprising it was formally subdivided in 1840 by Ralph Smith, a Haddonfield abolitionist, who renamed it Free Haven. Its name was changed to Lawnside in 1887 by the Philadelphia–Atlantic City Railroad when a train stop was established there. In 1926 Lawnside became the first

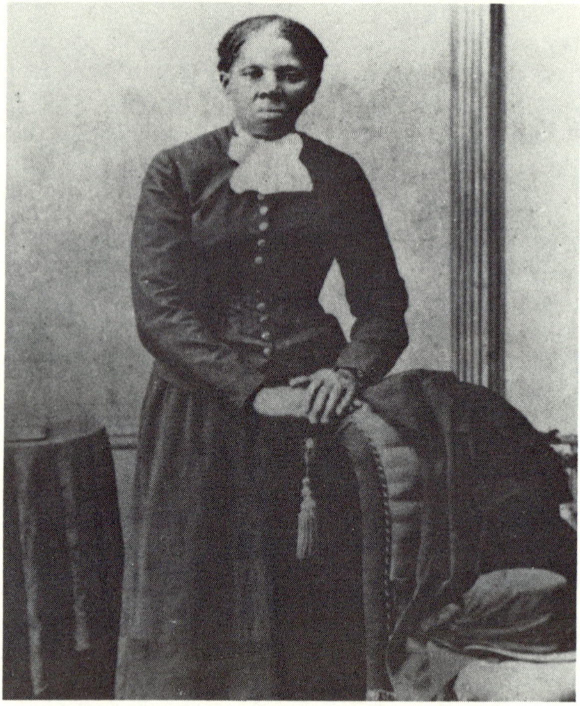

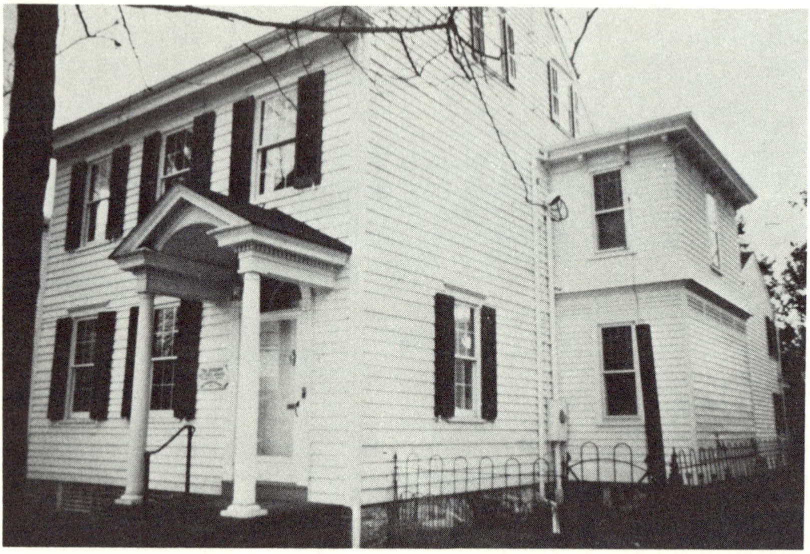

Above, left: Harriet Tubman (c. 1821-1913), fugitive slave, abolitionist, nurse, spy and social reformer, was the most famous conductor of the Underground Railroad. She made approximately nineteen trips into various slave states to lead some three hundred blacks out of bondage. She spent several periods of time in Cape May between 1849 and 1852, underscoring the strong connection between the Underground Railroad and New Jersey. Courtesy of the Smithsonian Institution.

Below, left: This house in Salem belonged to Abigail Goodwin (1794-1867) and her sister, Elizabeth. Abigail was a Quaker and one of New Jersey's leading abolitionists of the nineteenth century. The house, which still stands, is probably the only documented Underground Railroad station in New Jersey. Photograph collection of the New Jersey Historical Commission.

Above: Dr. James Still (1812-1885), born in Shamong, Burlington County, was one of the earliest black medical doctors in New Jersey. Mainly self-educated, he specialized in the preparation and use of traditional medicines such as powders, tinctures, salves, liniments, teas and vegetable oils. His success enabled him to acquire considerable property and to build a large house and office in Medford. His office still stands. Engraving in Early Recollections and Life of Dr. James Still *(Philadelphia, 1877), frontispiece.*

This is the first police force of the borough of Lawnside. The photo was taken in 1926, the year Lawnside became a municipality. It was the first historically all-black community in New Jersey to gain such status. Courtesy of Clarence Still.

black community in New Jersey to be incorporated as a municipality. It is today one of the few historically all-black towns in the nation that has this status. It had slightly over three thousand residents in 1980.

One constant for New Jersey blacks down to 1870 was their dim economic prospect. Throughout the state most blacks were concentrated at the bottom of the occupational hierarchy, in low-income, menial work. In southern New Jersey many farmed for themselves or worked as farm laborers, often on Quaker-owned farms and large estates. In the towns and cities with sizeable black populations, such as Newark, Trenton, Camden, Jersey City, Elizabeth and Princeton, they worked as unskilled laborers (for example, ditchdiggers, hod carriers and porters) or were engaged in the domestic and service trades. By 1870 the labor supply offered by white immigrants had reduced the position of blacks in the skilled crafts and precluded their employment in the industrial concerns that were springing up in the state's urban centers.

As early as 1808 African-American workers combined to protect themselves and to improve their economic situation. However, their early organizations functioned more as mutual aid societies and fraternal lodges, providing financial assistance in times of need, than as agents for bargaining with employers. During the 1860s blacks started to be admitted to white labor unions and to establish their own unions. In December 1869, in Washington, D. C., the first black national labor union federation was formed: the Colored National Labor Union. New Jersey was among the eighteen states represented at the founding meeting.

1870-1910

Two major developments shaped the New Jersey Afro-American experience for the next forty years. First, the number of black New Jerseyans almost tripled, mainly because of the arrival of southern blacks. In 1890, 43 per cent of New Jersey's blacks had been born in other states, and in 1910 the figure was 58 percent; corresponding figures for whites were 22 percent and 27 percent. Second, the black population became urbanized. By 1910 almost 75 percent of the state's black residents lived in cities.

That most of these urban areas were in the northern part of the state shows that southern migrants were beginning to shift away from the tendency to settle in South Jersey. Suburban Plainfield, the seashore resorts of Asbury Park and Long Branch, and the industrial cities of Elizabeth, Paterson and Jersey City had all experienced considerable growth in their black populations by 1910. The towns and cities of Essex County demonstrated the trend most clearly. Noticeable increases occurred in Montclair, Orange and East Orange, owing perhaps to their demand for domestic help, and the size of Newark's black population rose phenomenally. In 1910 Newark had almost ten thousand Afro-Americans, five times the nearly two thousand it had in 1870. As the state's most populous city, with an expanding economy, it could offer many positions traditionally occupied by blacks in the North—jobs for unskilled laborers, deliverymen, janitors, teamsters, laundresses, maids.

Only two sizable South Jersey communities—Camden and Atlantic City—drew significant black migratory streams between 1870 and

1910. Camden, which had the state's largest black population in 1880 and 1890, reached a little over six thousand in 1910, ranking third in the state. A far more spectacular change occurred in Atlantic City. Its black population increased from fifteen in 1870 to 9,834 in 1910, the largest in the state. It had a ratio of one black to five whites, the highest among sizable northern urban communities.

Atlantic City's rapid emergence as a major seaside resort explains the dramatic upsurge in its black population. The labor needed for the city's hotels and recreational facilities was largely black labor. The many service positions offered by the hotel-recreation industry—such as cook, waiter, bellman, porter, chambermaid—were within the occupational realm to which the black race had been customarily restricted. At the turn of the century the city's hotel-recreation labor force was 95 percent black.

The movement of southern blacks into South Jersey between 1870 and 1910 added one more all-black community: Whitesboro. Probably the last settlement of its kind established in New Jersey, it was named after George H. White of North Carolina, the last black congressman of the post-Reconstruction period. A group of blacks decided to leave Wilmington, North Carolina, after a race riot in 1898, and White helped them purchase land in Cape May County in 1899. By 1906 about three hundred families had settled in Whitesboro.

The 1870-1910 increase in the black population was accompanied by growth and changes in the social institutions that had traditionally forged cohesion among Afro-Americans. Religious bodies, for example, went through many changes. Older, pre-Civil War churches often rebuilt their edifices; the Bethel AME Church in Woodbury did so in 1874 and again in 1896, and Bordentown's Mt. Zion AME Church rebuilt in 1875. Others, such as Burlington's Wesley AME Church in 1893, built new quarters. Still others, like Burlington's Bethlehem AME Church in 1873, refurbished their existing edifices.

One early congregation became marked for fame through its association with the state's most illustrious black native son, Paul Robeson, the celebrated scholar, athlete, singer, actor, and civil rights activist. This was the Witherspoon Street Presbyterian Church in Princeton, which was established in 1837. Robeson's father, William Drew Robeson, served as its pastor between 1880 and 1902, and Paul was born in Princeton in 1898.

During these decades other churches opened their doors for the first time, often to serve the southern newcomers. Many of these were Baptist. In fact, most of the state's older black Baptist churches were

Paul Robeson (1898–1976), one of the major Afro-American figures of the twentieth century, has been described as a true Renaissance Man because of his many extraordinary talents. A native of Princeton, he also lived in Westfield and Somerville. He was graduated from Rutgers University in 1919 as class valedictorian. This photo was probably taken in the late 1930s. Courtesy of the Schomburg Center for Research in Black Culture, New York Public Library.

1870–1910

Since the 1840s social lodges have provided a meaningful form of group expression for Afro-Americans in New Jersey. Stressing exemplary conduct among their members, many of these bodies also performed benevolent functions. Members of Queen Esther Court No. 1 of Atlantic City (c. 1900) are shown above. Members of William S. Darr Lodge No. 3 of Camden (c. 1900) are pictured on the right. New Jersey Historical Commission.

established during this period: the Bethany Baptist Church in Newark (1871), perhaps the state's largest black congregation today; the Ebenezer Baptist Church in New Brunswick (1873); the Salem Baptist Church in Jersey City (1875); the Angelic Baptist Church in Bayonne (1887); the First African Baptist Church in Woodbridge (1905); and the First Baptist Church in Cranford (1910).

While the church continued to occupy its pivotal position in the black community, secular activities also increased and took new forms between 1870 and 1910. Some homes for the elderly and orphans were opened, and attempts began to establish YMCAs and YWCAs for Afro-Americans. Black fraternal orders became commonplace throughout the state. Many of the women's social clubs, which were to be united in 1915 in the New Jersey State Federation of Colored Women's Clubs, were formed. In some communities graduates of black colleges and universities organized alumni associations and local chapters of their Greek-letter fraternities and sororities.

The black press also developed between 1870 and 1910. Twelve papers were established, although only two survived until the turn of the century. Alfred R. Smith of Saddle River was perhaps the best-known black journalist of this period. During the 1880s and 1890s he was the publisher and editor of *The Landscape: A Country Newspaper.* In 1862, as a reporter for the Paterson *Guardian,* he had attracted attention by addressing an open letter protesting President Lincoln's support of a plan to solve the nation's racial problems by sending Afro-American volunteers to establish colonies in the Caribbean or Central America.

Some black-owned businesses that developed during this period experienced a better fate than the black press. Most were small enterprises that provided personal services—for example, barber shops, caterers, restaurants, and shoeshine parlors. There were also a few larger undertakings such as moving and storage businesses.

The masses of the race continued to occupy the lower rungs of the occupational ladder. In 1910 black urban males still tended to be laborers, deliverymen, janitors, porters, teamsters, chauffeurs, waiters and servants. Women were heavily employed as laundresses, dressmakers and domestic servants. The prejudice of white employers and employees combined to exclude blacks from factory work and the skilled crafts. Comments from labor and management in the 1903 Report of the Bureau of Statistics of Labor and Industries typify the mood of the period. "Their color and low instincts make them undesirable associates for white men," said an official of the carpenters' union in New Jersey. A representative of the glass bottle blowers declared, "[I] do not believe the average negro is capable of acquiring the skill necessary to become a successful glass blower. They are naturally lazy and are not clean in their habits." A New Jersey brick manufacturer stated, "[We] have no negroes employed at our works and have made no attempt to use negro labor. We prefer white foreign help such as Hungarians, Polanders, etc." And a manufacturer of hats observed, "We do not employ negroes in the hat manufacturing business; [we] do not believe they could be trained to do the work." Still, New Jersey blacks were part of the most significant labor organization of the 1880s: the Knights of Labor. Local assemblies of black Knights were established in Bridgeton and Camden.

Education remained a major concern. Between 1870 and 1910 the race was deeply divided in some communities over the question of integrated versus segregated public schools. As the public school system developed after 1871, cities in the northern counties—influenced, according to Marion Thompson Wright, by New York City—began to eliminate their racially separate schools. In 1881, however, a controversy arose in Fair Haven, Monmouth County, when blacks demanded the right to send their children to the white school. A school desegregation law enacted in that year was upheld by the state Supreme Court in 1884. The law protected children against being forced to attend schools according to race or nationality. As a consequence, almost all of the remaining separate schools in the northern counties were discontinued. However, the law did not prevent local school

Marion Thompson Wright (1904–1962), born in East Orange, was probably the first black female professional historian. Virtually all of her scholarly publications focused on some aspect of New Jersey Afro-American history. She taught at Howard University from 1940 until her death. Her interest in history led to a close relationship with Dr. Carter G. Woodson, considered the "Father of Afro-American History." This photograph dates from the late 1920s or early 1930s. Courtesy of James Moss.

officials from offering segregated facilities in the lower grades that might be voluntarily accepted. And certain black communities accepted such facilities. In fact, Fair Haven's blacks themselves finally chose a separate school.

In the southern counties the established black schools continued, and new ones were built. Their black opponents charged that they were inferior to white schools in physical facilities and quality of education. The blacks who supported them, however, considered them compatible with the advancement of the race because they provided a measure of autonomy and self-determination. Segregated schools, they noted, not only offered blacks teaching and administrative opportunities, but also spared black pupils the racial indignities often encountered in integrated classrooms.

As this debate continued, the system of all-black schools was encouraged in 1886 with the establishment of the New Jersey Manual Training and Industrial School for Colored Youth (better known as the "Bordentown School"). Its founder was a minister of the AME Church, the Reverend Walter A. Rice. Because it exemplified the educational philosophy of Booker T. Washington, it was known as the "Tuskegee of the North." It began in New Brunswick and was supported initially by voluntary public contributions. In 1894 it became a state-supported institution, and in 1896 it was moved to Bordentown. It operated until 1955. Its outstanding faculty included Lester B. Granger and Judge William Hastie, and its distinguished visitors (often commencement speakers) included Booker T. Washington, James Weldon Johnson, Paul Robeson, Mary McCleod Bethune, Albert Einstein and Eleanor Roosevelt. Increasingly, it faced criticism from those blacks who questioned the value of manual education as a solution to race problems and who opposed segregated public schools.

The New Jersey Manual Training and Industrial School for Colored Youth, an all-black northern high school whose students were boarders, was a unique educational institution. It placed a strong emphasis on discipline and order, and students were assigned chores that included work on the school's farm. The school was also a site for activities such as tournaments of the American Tennis Association, the black counterpart to the United States Lawn Tennis Association. The photographs on the right, taken in 1922, show students in the machine shop and the domestic science classroom. Courtesy of the Newark Public Library.

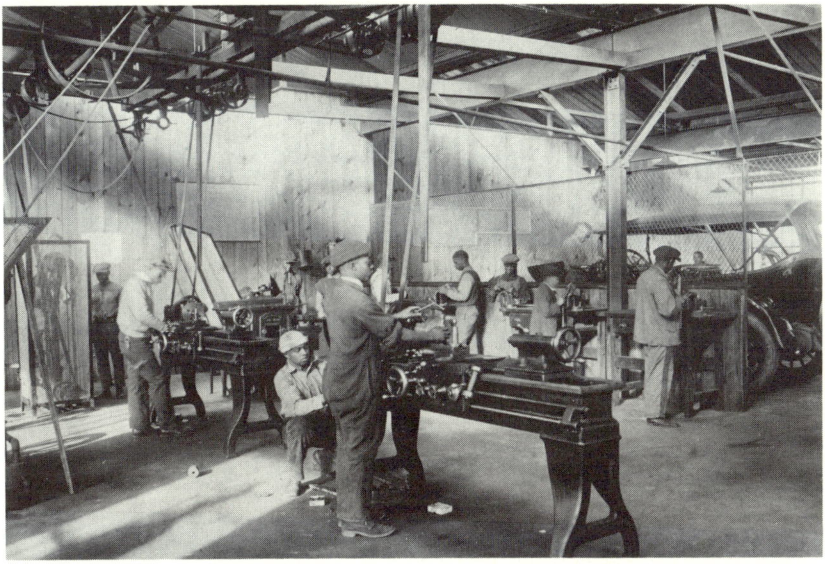

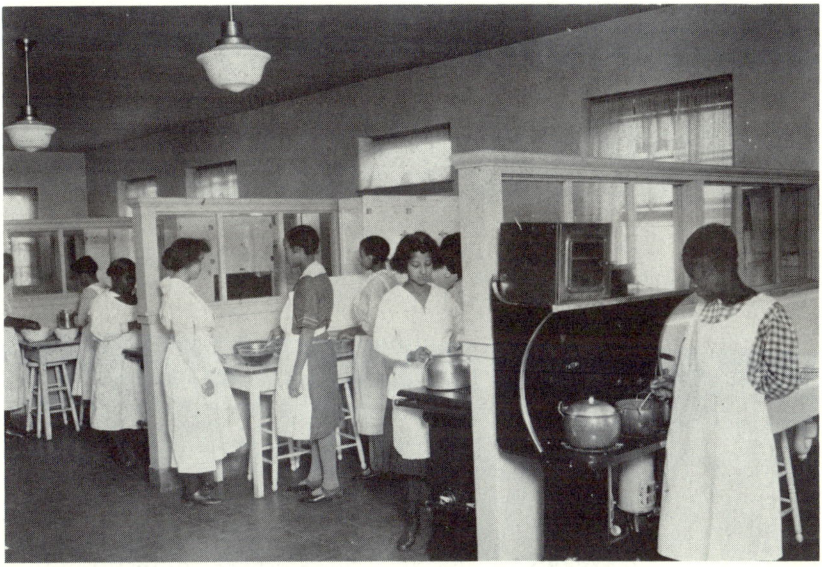

If some African-Americans were disheartened by the increase in segregated schools in the state between 1870 and 1910, virtually all welcomed the passage in 1884 of the state's first major civil rights law, which guaranteed all New Jerseyans equal access to public accommodations and jury service. Those violating anyone's civil rights were to be fined and required to pay damages to the victim. This law, however, was openly violated, particularly with respect to public accommodations. In 1917 it was revised and weakened to discourage suits by aggrieved persons. Damages were no longer awarded to the victims but to charitable institutions, and the complainants had no voice in selecting the recipients.

1910–1940

As noted earlier, a significant movement of Afro-Americans out of the South into New Jersey did not originate with World War I. Rather, the war, which began in 1914, is important for the state's Afro-American history because it prompted great numbers of southern blacks to settle in New Jersey in a brief period, and because their settlement had a tremendous impact both on their host communities and on themselves. For the first time, for example, blacks entered the state's manufacturing work force in substantial numbers. Lured mainly by the prospect of better-paying jobs, southern blacks began to migrate to New Jersey in unprecedented numbers around 1915, as part of a general trek northward.

By 1930 there were over two hundred thousand blacks in the state, a huge gain over the roughly eighty-eight thousand in 1910 (see Maps 6 and 7). Of the twenty-one northern cities in 1930 that had black populations over ten thousand, four—Newark, Atlantic City, Camden and Jersey City—were in New Jersey. Only Ohio, with seven, had more. The black New Jersey experience had become even more urban than before. And most of this growth was in the cities of North Jersey. The exceptions were Trenton, whose black population almost quadrupled from 1910 to 1930, and Atlantic City and Camden. Newark in particular received a disproportionate number of newcomers, showing a fourfold increase in black residents between 1910 and 1930.

As more Afro-Americans entered the state's cities and industrial labor force, increasing numbers of black workers participated in organized labor. Blacks in longshore work and the clothing industry (including women workers) were among those organized. In 1917 Pros-

1910–1940

Because of the poor living and working conditions attendant to sharecropping, many Afro-Americans left the South during the first sixty-odd years of the twentieth century and moved to northern states in search of a better life. This photograph (c. 1915) shows a sharecropper and his family, their living quarters, and the cotton field they worked. The white man in the background is probably the owner of the plantation they lived on. Courtesy of the Balch Institute.

per Brewer led a strike of black dock workers at Port Newark which ended with a wage increase. In the dramatic and violent textile strike of 1926, involving the woolen mills of Passaic, Clifton, Garfield and Lodi, blacks were not only among the strikers, but four served as delegates on the strike committee and one was vice-chairman of the strikers' executive committee. In a strike in 1923 at the Sayre-Fisher brickmaking plant in Sayreville, blacks played a different role. The Newark Urban League recruited them to serve as strikebreakers, reflecting the long-standing hostility of many black middle-class leaders toward organized labor, especially the craft unions, because of discriminatory admission practices.

The Afro-Americans who arrived during the Great Migration laid the foundation for the state's black ghettos. Before this heavy influx, urban blacks lived mainly in scattered enclaves. But as the large

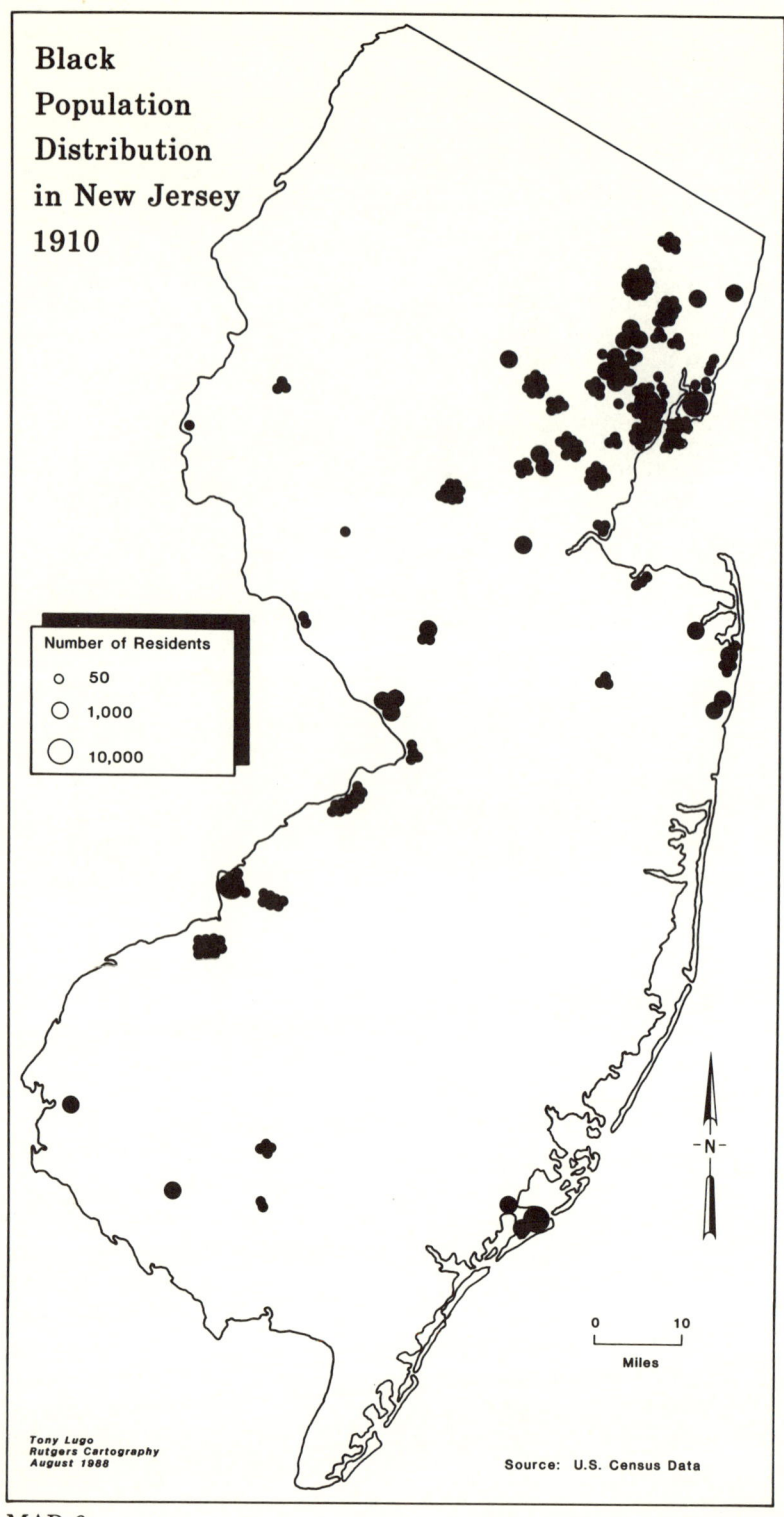

Black Population Distribution in New Jersey 1910

Number of Residents
- 50
- 1,000
- 10,000

Tony Lugo
Rutgers Cartography
August 1988

Source: U.S. Census Data

0   10
Miles

MAP 6

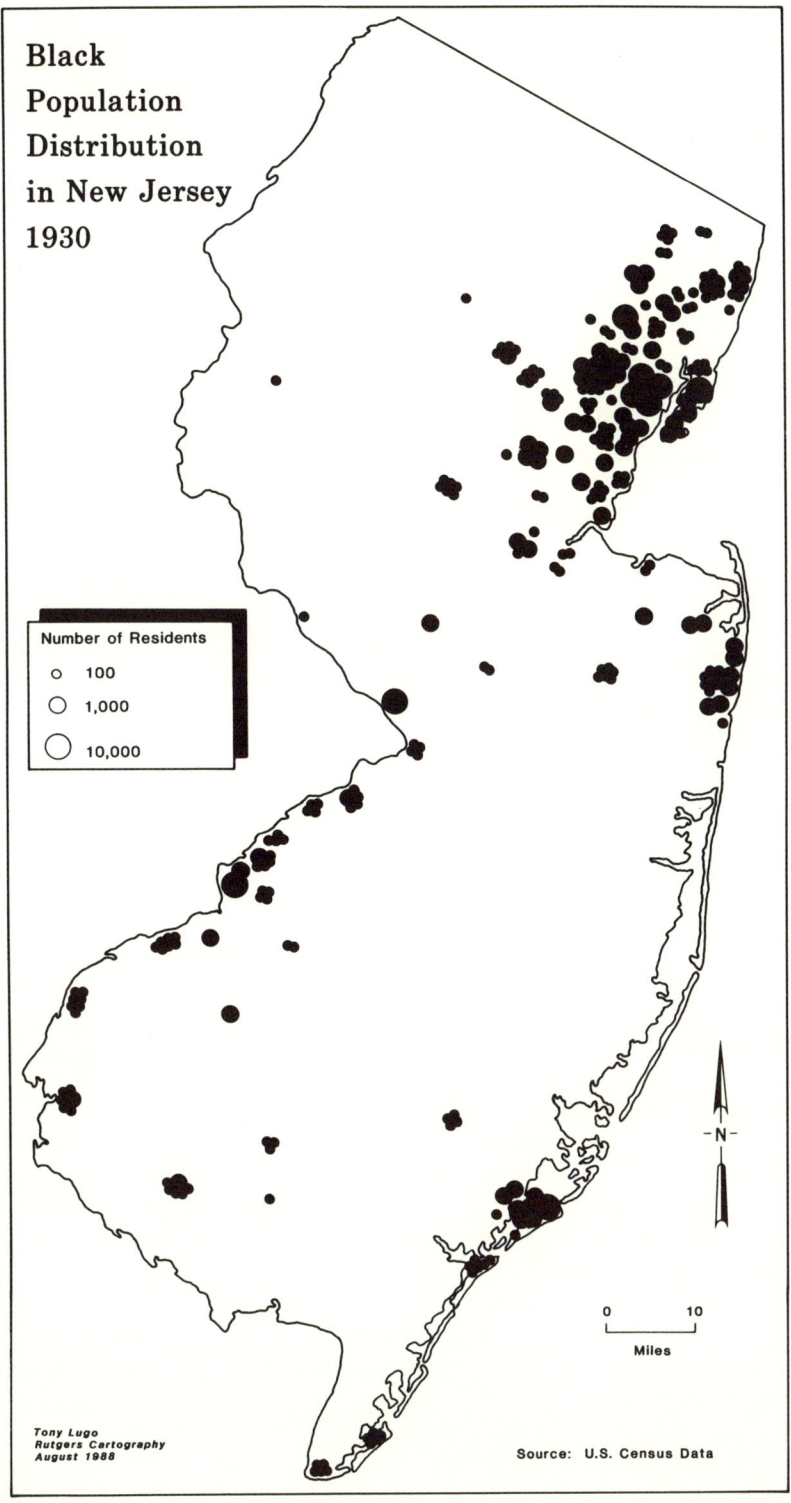

Black Population Distribution in New Jersey 1930

Number of Residents
- ○ 100
- ○ 1,000
- ◯ 10,000

Tony Lugo
Rutgers Cartography
August 1988

Source: U.S. Census Data

MAP 7

Dry-cleaning establishments, like this one in Newark (c. 1930s), offered migrants higher pay than they normally received in the South. Courtesy of Henrietta Parker.

numbers of newcomers encountered discriminatory housing practices, a new residential pattern emerged. Large concentrations of blacks developed in one or two sections of a city. Compared to the various European immigrant groups with whom they shared the cities, blacks generally experienced greater residential segregation. Not only did they tend to be more sharply segregated from other ethnic groups than those groups were from each other, but their residential isolation tended to increase over time while that of other ethnic groups lessened. Economic advancement, for example, did not free African-Americans from confinement to black residential areas; when they moved into previously all-white areas, those areas invariably turned black. In addition, the economic opportunities generated for blacks by World War I gradually disappeared during the 1920s. The now familiar signs of ghetto life began to appear: poverty, unemployment, dilapidated and overcrowded housing at high cost, inadequate sanitation and poor health standards.

The sizable presence of southern black newcomers gave rise to many new institutions and organizations that were essential to the survival and integrity of the ghetto communities. The storefront church appeared, with a unique religious style that appealed to many migrants. In contrast to the older churches, it provided a more emotional and intense form of worship in a smaller and more personal setting.

Religious sects were also a part of the new social order. One of the most secretive was the Moorish Science Temple of America, which was formed in Newark in 1913 by Noble Drew Ali, a self-proclaimed prophet who had migrated to Newark from North Carolina. Ali later moved to Chicago and established a national Moorish Science Temple, from which Elijah Muhammad's Nation of Islam eventually emerged.

The Peace Mission Movement of Father Divine, which flourished during the Depression of the 1930s, attracted a considerable following among black New Jerseyans, especially in Newark. During the 1930s

The creation of storefront churches was one result of the Great Migration. Such churches enabled migrants to continue a style of religious worship they had practiced in the South. This church was in Newark in the 1930s. Courtesy of the New Jersey Division of Archives and Records Management.

the movement established several small businesses there and owned a fairly large building.

As the ghettos grew, more Afro-Americans were able to heed the age-old exhortations of black leaders and newspapers to go into business for themselves. Indeed, most of the state's black urban communities came to feature an array of black-owned establishments that catered mainly to blacks: building and loan associations, hotels, beauty parlors, dry cleaning shops, printing shops, funeral parlors, photography shops, pool halls, saloons, laundries, realty companies, employment agencies, shoe repair shops, confectioneries, butcher shops, ice houses, and dressmaking shops. The most successful tended to be barber shops, beauty parlors, restaurants, pool halls, and undertakers, which met needs normally ignored by white businesses in the ghetto. In contrast, small retail businesses owned by blacks were often unable to offer a wide variety of products and extend credit to customers, whereas their white competitors had the capital to offer these options to buyers.

The Apex Beauty Products Company in Atlantic City, a hair cosmetics firm, was by far the largest and most significant of New Jersey's black-owned businesses during this period. Established in 1919 by Sara Spencer Washington, it became one of the nation's leading black manufacturing companies. By the late 1930s its Atlantic City office and factory had eighty-seven employees, including chemists, clerks, bookkeepers, chauffeurs and beauty operators. The company also had eleven beauty schools in various cities. An estimated thirty-five thousand individuals throughout the world were dependent on the sales of its products and its method of "Scientific Beauty Culture."

The expanded ghetto economy also facilitated an increase of black professionals: teachers, physicians, nurses, dentists, lawyers, pharmacists and social workers. While the Great Migration's participants were largely poor and low in status, professionals also participated in the exodus north. Many of them helped organize such bodies as the New Jersey Association for Teachers of Colored Children, the Commonwealth Dental Association, and the North Jersey Medical Society.

The black press too benefited from the influx, and by 1940 over thirty black newspapers had been founded. Among the better known were the *Record,* the *Afro-American,* and the state's most widely circulated black weekly, the *New Jersey Herald News* (later the *Newark Herald News*). Aside from representing the black business

Sara Spencer Washington (1889–1953), founder of the Apex Beauty Products Company, was one of New Jersey's leading Afro-American entrepreneurs of the first half of the twentieth century. When she died her estate was worth over one million dollars. She also left an impressive record of involvement in social, civic, and political activities. Courtesy of the Schomburg Center for Research in Black Culture, New York Public Library.

interests that supported them financially, the black papers kept the community abreast of newsworthy events and continued the tradition of articulating the concerns, grievances and aspirations of the race.

No institutions affected by the Great Migration grew so rapidly as those meeting social and recreational needs. In most instances these organizations provided the only significant opportunity for group expression aside from the church. They included social clubs, whose activities ranged from card playing to handicrafts; cultural groups such as glee clubs, art clubs, drama societies, and "Negro History" clubs; veterans' groups, including the American Legion and the Veterans of Foreign Wars; youth groups such as the Boy Scouts and the Girl Scouts; and such civic groups as the United Civic and Welfare League of Plainfield, the Citizens' Civic League of Pleasantville, the North Jersey Civic Association of Newark and the Citizens' Civic Welfare League of New Brunswick.

Perhaps the most important organizations were the black lodges—the Masons, Odd Fellows, Elks, Knights of Pythias, American Woodmen, Sons and Daughters of Africa, Order of Moses, Good Samaritans, Eastern Star, Queen Esther Court, Court of Calanthe, Household of Ruth, and others. These bodies gave leadership opportunities and offered social and civic betterment through college scholarships, charity drives, volunteer services, and other programs. Many of them provided sick and death benefits for members. They also worked for the moral and social uplift of the race by promoting the development of strong individual character and stressing exemplary behavior.

Some organizations sought to advance the interests of the race by working for civil rights and challenging segregation and other symbols of racial intolerance. Most conspicuous were the National Association for the Advancement of Colored People (NAACP), organized in 1909, and the National Urban League, founded in 1911. The NAACP used litigation to fight racial barriers, especially in education and places of public accommodation. The Urban League aimed mainly at helping southern migrants adjust to the North, particularly in acquiring suitable employment and housing. Some of the early chapters of those organizations were established in New Jersey. The Orange NAACP, organized in 1913, was the first in the state, followed by the Newark NAACP in 1914. The Newark Urban League was created in 1919, an outgrowth of the Negro Welfare League, which had been established in 1917.

Marcus Garvey's Universal Negro Improvement Association

(UNIA) offered a contrasting ideology and style of protest. A black nationalist who emphasized racial pride, Garvey bitterly opposed what he considered the integrationist approach of the NAACP and the Urban League. He summoned Afro-Americans to a program of "African Redemption" that included resettlement in Africa. There were over thirty UNIA divisions in New Jersey, not only in cities like Newark, Jersey City, Trenton, Camden, and Atlantic City, but also in the smaller communities of Montclair, Vauxhall, Kenilworth, Burlington, Glassboro and Whitesboro. Garvey was imprisoned for mail fraud in 1925 and was deported to his native Jamaica in late 1927. The UNIA went into decline. Its ranks dwindled further during the Great Depression, as hard times forced Afro-Americans to look to their own immediate survival rather than to ambitious and far-reaching plans for global race betterment.

Of all New Jersey ethnic groups, Afro-Americans suffered most during the Depression of the 1930s. In 1932 black unemployment in the state was nearly twice that of whites. And once blacks lost their jobs they tended to remain unemployed longer than whites, so that they were more likely to become impoverished. In 1935 26 per cent of the families on relief in the state were black, although black families constituted only five per cent of the state's total family population. In 1937 the relief rolls in the state's eight largest cities revealed a disproportionate number of blacks; they were three to six times more likely to be relief recipients than whites in these cities. In Elizabeth, for example, where blacks constituted 4.2 per cent of the family population, they accounted for 28.5 per cent of the family relief cases.

Black worker displacement was another feature of the Depression. White workers drove blacks out of certain positions they had held for decades. Waiters, hotel workers, elevator operators and others were replaced by young white women, while janitors and others were supplanted by white men.

The radically depressed wages associated with the nation's most severe economic downturn provided greater opportunities for employer exploitation of black workers. Among domestic workers it led to unprecedented humiliation—to what contemporary observers called "slave markets." In these "markets," black women waited on street corners for white women to drive up, casually survey them, and then offer them a day's work.

The Great Depression also reduced the overall volume of southern black migration appreciably. However, it considerably increased the flow of southern black migratory workers into southern and central

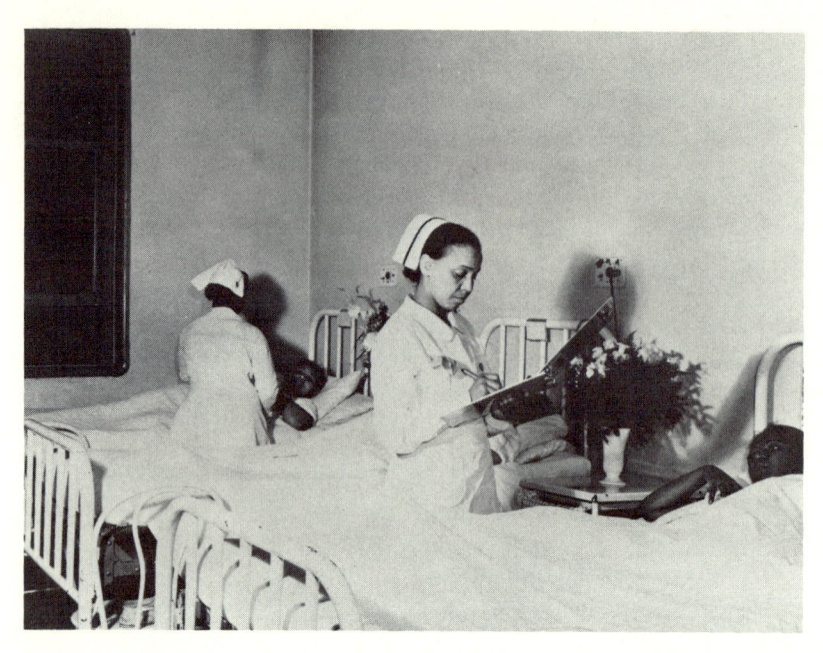

Newark's black community was large enough to establish and sustain certain kinds of institutions in the face of racial discrimination. The photos above and top right (c. 1930s) show the medical staff of the Community Hospital of Newark, which was established in 1927. The lower photo shows the National Theater of Newark. Courtesy of the New Jersey Division of Archives and Records Management.

New Jersey. This flow had been reported as early as 1892, when blacks from Virginia, Maryland, and North Carolina were identified as seasonal workers on farms in South Jersey. Many of those who entered New Jersey in the 1930s had been displaced by the mechanization of cotton production and by the cotton acreage reduction programs in effect during the 1930s. They replaced Italians, who often worked as family units, in harvesting the state's fruit, berry and produce crops. Drawn principally from the Eastern seaboard, many of these black workers began their cycle in Florida in the spring and worked in South Carolina, North Carolina and Virginia before reaching New Jersey in the summer. At the height of the season in 1940, they totaled

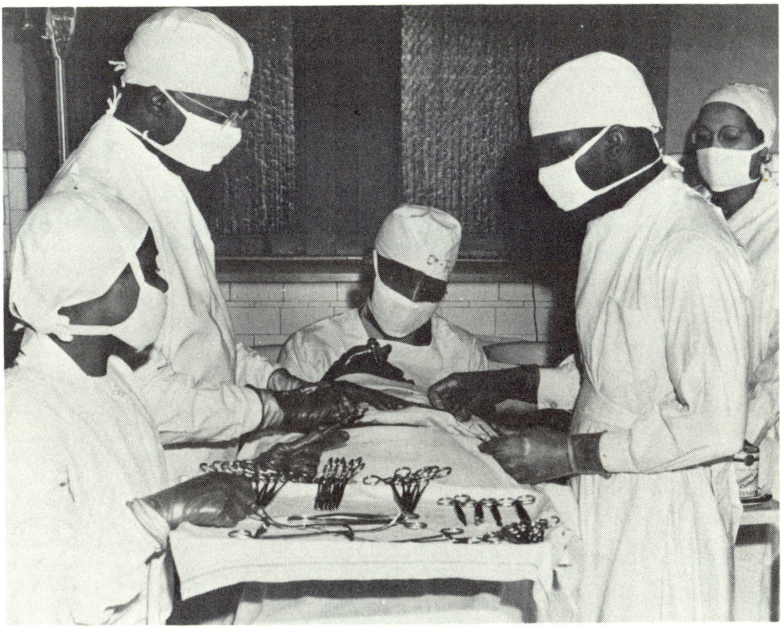

SUN. MON. TUES.
THE STORY OF
GEORGE WASHINGTON CARVER
JANE
High School
It's COMFORTABLY COOL inside
JANE WYMAN DICK FORAN
NATIONAL

about ten thousand. Over four thousand were employed on the potato, fruit and vegetable farms of Mercer, Monmouth and Middlesex counties in that year alone. By the mid-1960s, Puerto Ricans had generally replaced these southern blacks.

The New Deal labor legislation of July 1935 affirmed the right of workers to organize. This gave rise to an attempt by the Congress of Industrial Organizations (CIO), which had developed from the Committee for Industrial Organization formed in November 1935, to organize the nation's industrial labor force. Black workers in New Jersey had achieved a more diversified presence in this force despite the Depression. They were found in appreciable numbers in the steel, shipbuilding, and other industries where the CIO carried out organizing drives. The CIO's rival, the American Federation of Labor (AFL), despite its tradition of illiberal racial policies, also had Afro-Ameri-

New Jersey is one of the states in the Northeast to which black migrant workers from as far south as Florida come each year to labor on vegetable and fruit farms. This photograph dates from 1940 and was taken in Sawboro, North Carolina. Its original caption indicated that these workers were from Florida and were on their way to "Cranberry" (sic), New Jersey, to harvest potatoes. Courtesy of the Library of Congress.

This photograph (c. 1940s) shows black migrant workers sacking potatoes on a farm in Cranbury. The oppressive and exploitative conditions under which migrant workers have labored in New Jersey have been compared with the worst features of the sharecropping system in the South. Courtesy of the Newark Public Library.

cans in its ranks in the state. By the late 1930s black hod carriers, oystermen, teamsters, musicians and a few others were members of New Jersey AFL affiliates.

The economic distress of the Great Depression was accompanied by a growth in black political assertiveness and grass-roots protest. In the state's larger cities, for example, "Buy Where You Can Work" boycotts were organized to pressure white-owned businesses in black communities to integrate their work forces. Rent strikes for better housing were also conducted in these cities, as well as efforts to block the eviction of neighbors for failing to pay their rent. Other collective activities with which blacks defended themselves against the Depression were "rent parties" and the sharing and bartering of goods such as foods and services such as hairdressing.

During the Depression the political allegiance of Afro-Americans changed dramatically. Influenced by the Civil War, Lincoln's Emancipation Proclamation and the Reconstruction period, blacks had for years solidly supported the Republican Party. It was the only major party that offered them a modicum of political power before the 1930s. Dr. George E. Cannon, a physician from Jersey City, for example, was active in the party at the city, county, state and national levels; as a delegate to the Republican National Convention in 1924 he seconded the nomination of Calvin Coolidge. When, thanks to the Great Migration, blacks reached sufficient numerical strength to start electing public officials in New Jersey, the first winners were Republicans. Walter G. Alexander of Orange, the first black member of the state legislature, was elected to the general assembly as a Republican in 1921. In the next decade he was followed by other black Republicans from Essex County.

During the 1930s blacks shifted to the Democratic Party, and in 1937 Guy Moorehead of Newark became the first black Democrat to serve in the assembly. The identification of the Democratic Party with the New Deal and the egalitarian vision of Franklin Delano Roosevelt were instrumental in this change in allegiance. The social welfare measures with which the New Deal addressed the hardships of the Great Depression were especially well received by the black community.

Between 1910 and 1940 the number of separate black schools continued to increase. From 1919 to 1930 it grew from fifty-two to sixty-six, and there were seventy black schools by 1935. On the eve of World War II, from Princeton south every city or town with an appreciable black population supported a dual system of elementary schools. A report submitted to the state legislature in 1939 deplored much about this system. Most commonly white pupils were taught in larger and more modern facilities than black students, and in some cases blacks were not even given the minimum essentials for adequate instruction—books, maps, gymnasium facilities, shop equipment. In a less common arrangement whites and blacks shared a school but had separate classrooms and sometimes separate entrances, toilets and playgrounds.

1940–1980s

World War II lifted the nation out of the Great Depression. It created a general shortage of workers that made many war-related

1940-1980s

Whereas southern states virtually excluded Afro-Americans from voting until the mid-1960s, New Jersey did not. This photograph shows blacks voting at the Prince Charlton School in Newark in the 1930s. During this decade Afro-Americans shifted their allegiance from the Republican Party to the Democratic Party. Courtesy of the New Jersey Division of Archives and Records Management.

industrial jobs available to Afro-Americans. These jobs offered wages that were high compared to those of the Depression days, and some also provided an opportunity to upgrade skills. A much higher percentage of black women joined the industrial work force than in World War I. Most of them left some form of domestic service.

The war also triggered a new surge of migrants to the state, as once again black southerners formed an industrial labor reserve. Like the earlier newcomers of the Great Migration, they tended to settle in the larger municipalities—Camden, Trenton and such northern urban centers as Newark, Jersey City, Paterson, East Orange and Elizabeth.

Finally, because the war involved a struggle against racist and antidemocratic forces abroad, it created a climate that strengthened the resolve of New Jersey blacks to struggle against racial injustice at home. In some ways a new era dawned in the state's race relations. According to Marion Thompson Wright, New Jersey "blazed trails in the improvement of human relations." With the assistance of whites who were committed to social justice, Afro-Americans achieved increased civil rights in the immediate postwar years.

In 1945 the state passed a Fair Employment Practices Act that forbade racial discrimination in employment. A Division Against Discrimination was established in the Department of Education to administer the act; this was the first state agency established to eliminate racial and ethnic discrimination. In 1949, with the strong support of Republican Governor Alfred E. Driscoll, the 1945 law was revised to prohibit discrimination in public accommodations. The Freeman Act of 1949 enabled victims of racial or ethnic discrimination to file complaints with the Division Against Discrimination. Further legislation in 1954 prohibited racial discrimination in public housing.

Another postwar achievement in the African-American community's battle against racism can be found in the state's third constitution, adopted in 1947. It outlawed racial segregation in the public schools and the state militia. As the first state to make such provisions constitutionally, New Jersey altered its image of racial conservatism. More important, for the first time black pupils and teachers in the southern counties were placed in schools and classes on a nonracial basis. The integration of the New Jersey militia was among the catalysts for similar action by the Truman administration that led to the desegregation of the nation's armed forces.

Blacks continued to arrive from the South in droves during the immediate postwar period. All told, the state's black population increased by 40 percent during and after the war, from 226,973 in 1940 to 318,565 in 1950—close to 7 percent of the population.

In the second half of the twentieth century the pace of southern black movement to New Jersey quickened, and it did not abate until around the end of the 1960s. Afro-Americans became much more visible in the populations of certain industrial cities like Paterson, Passaic and New Brunswick. Between 1950 and 1970 the state's black population more than doubled. And by 1980 the 924,786 blacks in the state constituted almost 13 percent of the population, the highest percentage ever (see Map 8).

The increased presence of blacks in New Jersey was keenly felt in urban areas. By 1980 the Afro-American population was over 95

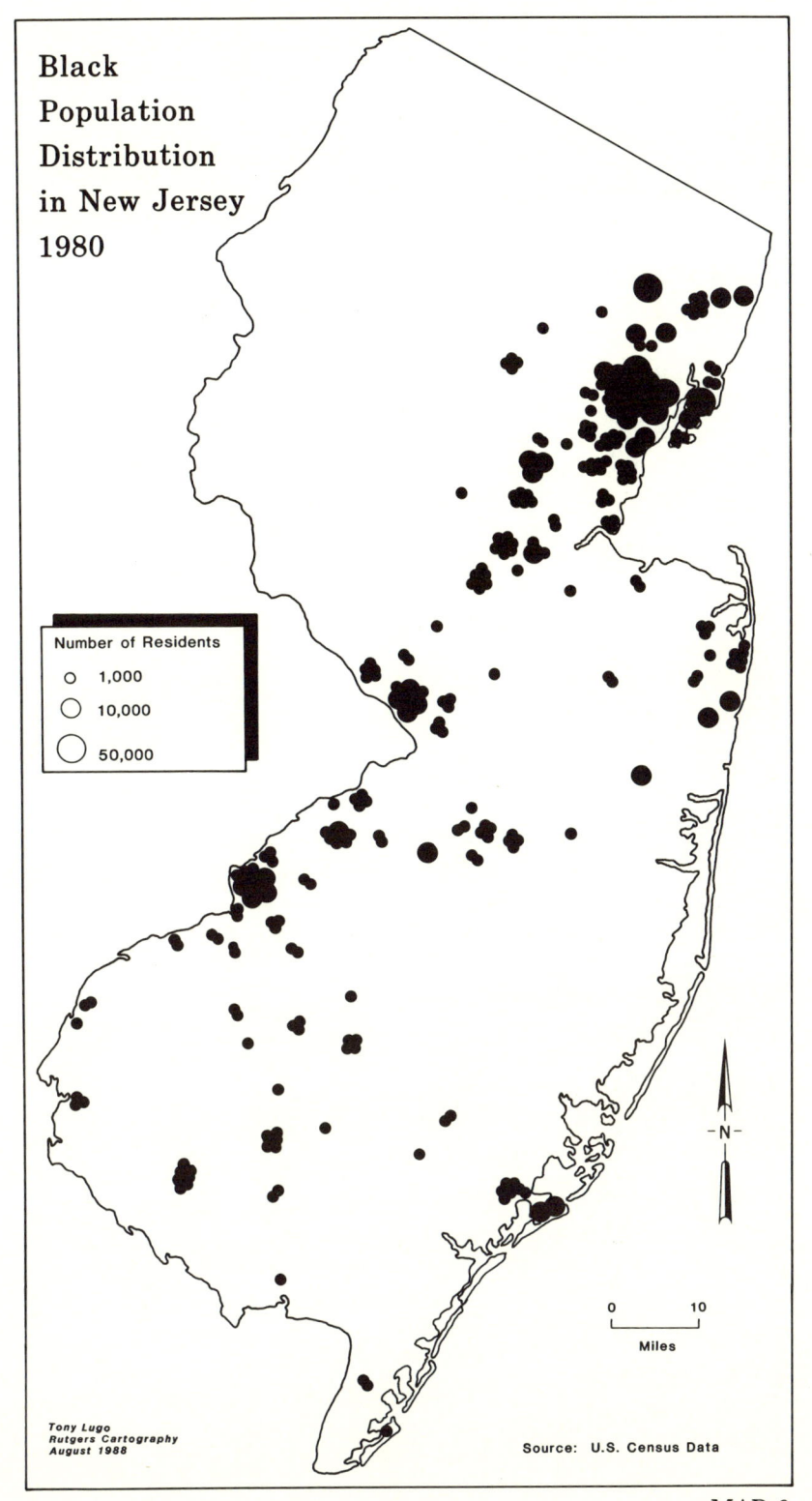

Black Population Distribution in New Jersey 1980

Number of Residents
- ○ 1,000
- ○ 10,000
- ○ 50,000

Tony Lugo
Rutgers Cartography
August 1988

Source: U.S. Census Data

0   10
Miles

MAP 8

percent urban and was centered in the northern part of the state. Six virtually contiguous communities in North Jersey—Newark, East Orange, Orange, Elizabeth, Irvington and Jersey City—had over forty percent of the state's black population.

As the numbers of blacks in the urban areas grew, several developments occurred that were to undermine gains made during World War II. One was the spread of the ghettos, which was accelerated especially as whites, encouraged by federal highway and housing policies, began fleeing to the suburbs during the 1950s. Another was the increasing economic depression among ghetto dwellers. Many of the factory jobs that had initially attracted blacks from the South were lost as companies mechanized and automated their plants or moved them to other parts of the country and abroad, and as the economy shifted from industry to services.

By the mid-1960s new problems had been added to ghetto life. For example, fewer black men were participating in the labor force, and de facto segregated schools developed with low levels of academic achievement and high dropout rates. Such manifestations of racial inequality, against a backdrop of rising expectations, caused some of the state's larger black communities to erupt in violence in the 1960s. During the early part of the decade, Jersey City, Elizabeth and Paterson experienced rioting by blacks. Later, major riots occurred in Newark, Plainfield and Englewood, and lesser ones broke out in Trenton, Camden, Paterson, Atlantic City and New Brunswick. The Newark riot of July 1967, which brought out the State Police and the National Guard, was one of the most severe civil disturbances of the decade. Property damage exceeded $10 million, and twenty-three persons died. Only the riots in the Watts section of Los Angeles (1965) and in Detroit (1967), cities with much larger black populations, involved more fatalities. Thirty-four died in Los Angeles, forty in Detroit.

Afro-Americans in the state were also involved in other forms of protest in the 1960s. A militant black community consciousness, often called "Black Power," was embraced by urban activists. Amiri Baraka (born Everette LeRoi Jones), the poet, writer and playwright, was at the vortex of militant black cultural and nationalist activities. When he returned to his native Newark in late 1965, he placed the city in the forefront of radical protest efforts. In 1967, for example, a National Conference on Black Power was convened there.

The cry of "Black Power!" was also heard in the labor movement. In April 1967, for example, five hundred black workers shut down

1940–1980s

The prospect of well-paid industrial jobs continued to lure southern black workers to New Jersey well into the 1960s. However, during this decade the number of such jobs, for a variety of reasons, began to decline in New Jersey, causing a rise in black unemployment. This photograph (c. 1950s) shows blacks working in the steel section of the Worthington Corporation plant in Harrison. Courtesy of Newark Public Library.

production at the Ford Motor Company plant at Mahwah for three days because a foreman addressed a worker with a racial epithet. After the foreman was removed and the wildcat strike ended, the United Black Workers of Mahwah Ford was organized. It maintained relations with the League of Revolutionary Black Workers, an organization of black workers' caucuses at auto plants in the Detroit area.

Black New Jerseyans were also involved in civil rights protest. Beginning shortly after World War II and lasting to the late 1960s, African-Americans, often under the leadership of the NAACP, engaged in successful efforts to eliminate discrimination in public restaurants, hotels, theaters, parks, and other accommodations in communities throughout the state. In addition, some became supporters of the modern civil rights movement that emerged in the South in the 1950s; they embraced the nonviolent protest philosophy of Dr. Martin Luther King, Jr., and often contributed financially to the movement. Dr. King himself was no stranger to New Jersey; New Jerseyans such as Rabbi Joachim Prinz of Newark and the Reverend S. Howard Woodson, Jr., pastor of the Shiloh Baptist Church of Trenton, knew him intimately. Dr. King visited New Jersey about a week before his death to mobilize support for his Poor People's Campaign. On March 27, 1968, he made several daytime appearances in Newark, briefly met with Amiri Baraka, and spoke in the evening at church rallies in Newark, Paterson, Orange and Jersey City. He was assassinated April 4 in Memphis.

Black protest of the 1950s and 1960s helped bring about the Johnson Administration's national War on Poverty, much civil rights legislation, and other reforms during the 1960s. It also created greater opportunities for black New Jerseyans, bringing unprecedented numbers into the mainstream of society. Job training programs, for example, enabled some blacks to acquire meaningful employment for the first time. More blacks entered governmental units where the race had been barely visible, such as the state police. Afro-Americans made noticeable gains in professional, managerial and technical positions. The black presence grew on city councils and school boards. Blacks began to occupy high and powerful political posts. A notable example was Kenneth Gibson, who in 1970 was elected the first black mayor of Newark. Three years later, the Reverend S. Howard Woodson, Jr., became the first black speaker of the state assembly, the first of his race to occupy such a position in any state since Reconstruction. Also, as discriminatory housing practices lessened, a growing number of black New Jerseyans became suburbanites, adding another dimension to the history of black migration. Finally, owing to special criteria and programs created to encourage enrollment, Afro-Americans entered the state's colleges, universities and medical, dental and law schools in unprecedented numbers.

Since the 1960s some of these gains have eroded, and many of the state's blacks remain mired in poverty. Statistically a grim portrait can be drawn of much of contemporary New Jersey Afro-American life. Using various indices of poverty, analysts have declared two predominantly black New Jersey municipalities—Camden and Newark—the poorest in the nation for their size; as a result they have been greatly maligned and treated as metaphors for urban squalor and decay. In 1983 black families had a poverty rate of 24.9 percent and were about four times more likely than white families to live below the poverty level as defined by the federal government; median family income was $16,384 for blacks and $31,851 for whites. In 1985 the black unemployment rate was 12.6 percent, more than twice the 4.8 percent for whites. This differential remained constant from 1980. In 1984 only 40.3 percent of black children lived with both parents, compared to 82.7 percent of white children. Recent figures indicate that the number of black full-time undergraduates in New Jersey colleges and universities decreased by 7.9 percent between 1983 and 1984 and by another 8 percent—from 15,473 to 14,242—the next year. And while blacks made up a little over 13 percent of the state's total population in 1985, they constituted 61 percent of its prison population.

Yet there is another dimension to New Jersey Afro-American life since the 1960s. Some of the state's blacks have achieved success, and they are faring better in the 1980s than they were one or two decades ago. They have a life style much like that of other middle-class Americans. In recent years their proportion has increased slightly: in 1980 about 29 percent of all black families earned more than the state median income of $22,900, whereas in 1970 only about 27 percent exceeded the state median of $11,400. One factor in this development was the increased employment of blacks in professional, technical, managerial and administrative jobs between 1970 and 1980. In 1980, for example, 7.9 percent of all professionals and technicians in the state were black, as compared to 4.9 percent in 1970.

As we move closer to the twenty-first century, therefore, there are developments that are both encouraging and disturbing. It is cause for hope, for example, that more Afro-Americans have assumed judicial and political authority and responsibility. Nine Afro-Americans sit on the Superior Court bench. Eight are members of the state legislature; two of these are women, following in the footsteps of Assemblywoman Madeline A. Williams of East Orange, who in 1957 was the first black woman elected to the legislature. There are black mayors of such major cities as Camden, East Orange, Plainfield, Atlantic City and Newark, and Afro-American members of the Governor's cabinet. And in 1988 the first black Congressman from New Jersey was elected.

On the other hand, there has been an alarming social transformation in the urban black ghettos, where certain problems have reached unprecedented dimensions. For example, drug use has proliferated, crime has risen, and more and more households are without male adults. These, added to other social dislocations that characterize much of black urban existence, suggest that a significant

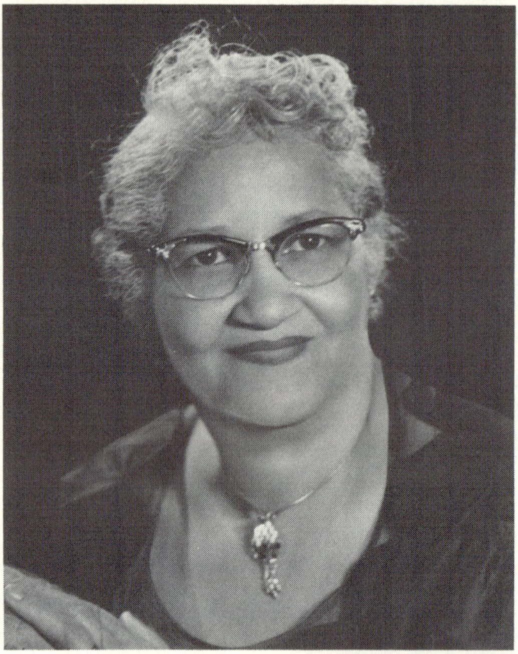

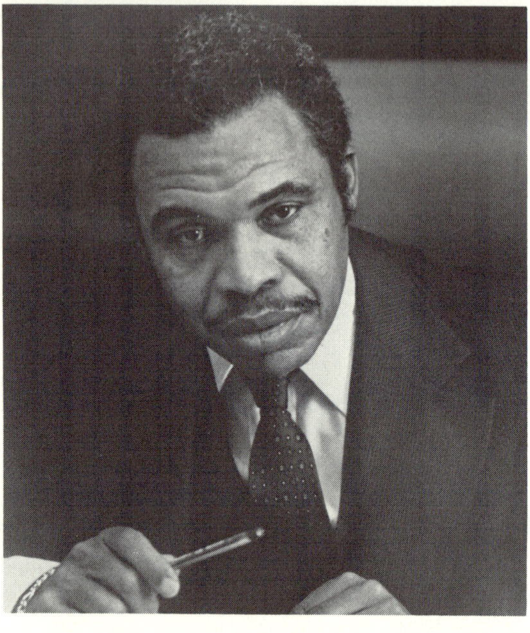

portion of the black community is isolated from the broader economic and social life of the state. Thus, some experts perceive an increasing polarization of the black race in New Jersey. On one side they see a growing middle class, enjoying the benefits of gains in civil rights, politics, housing, social status and wage equality. On the other hand, there is an almost unshrinkable segment of blacks unable to take advantage of the same gains and locked in a cycle of poverty. This polarization casts in a new light the paradox of New Jersey Afro-American life.

To a state that has made considerable progress in race relations, and to a race that has overcome formidable obstacles in the past, the poor, unemployed and undereducated blacks of the cities pose a new challenge. They challenge the state to call upon its considerable resources to accord all of its Afro-American citizens an existence consistent with their hopes and aspirations. They challenge the black community to draw on its traditional resilience and resourcefulness and its history of struggle for self-betterment.

Madeline A. Williams (1896-1968) of East Orange was the first black woman elected to the New Jersey legislature. She was elected to the General Assembly in 1957 as a Democrat. Earlier she taught in the Trenton school system for eight years. Active in a number of social, civic and civil rights organizations, she took particular legislative interest in child labor, child welfare, juvenile delinquency and migrant labor. Courtesy of the Newark Public Library.

Kenneth Gibson (1932-) in 1970 became the first of his race to be elected mayor of New Jersey's largest city, Newark. This photograph dates from 1981, when he unsuccessfully sought the Democratic Party's nomination for governor of the state. Courtesy of the Newark Public Library.

Appendixes

APPENDIX 1

BLACK POPULATION GROWTH IN NEW JERSEY SINCE 1870

YEAR	TOTAL	PERCENTAGE OF INCREASE
1870	30,658	—
1880	38,853	26.7
1890	47,638	22.6
1900	69,844	46.6
1910	89,760	28.5
1920	117,132	30.5
1930	208,828	78.3
1940	226,973	8.7
1950	318,565	40.4
1960	514,875	61.6
1970	770,292	49.6
1980	925,066	20.1

APPENDIXES

APPENDIX 2

BLACK POPULATION IN NEW JERSEY SINCE 1790

YEAR	TOTAL POPULATION	BLACKS	SLAVES	PERCENTAGE OF BLACKS IN SLAVERY
1790	184,139	14,185	11,423	80.5
1800	211,149	16,824	12,422	73.8
1810	245,555	18,694	10,851	58.0
1820	277,575	20,012	7,557	37.8
1830	320,823	20,557	2,254	11.0
1840	373,306	21,718	684	3.1
1850	489,555	24,046	236	1.0
1860	672,035	25,336	18	*
1870	906,096	30,658		
1880	1,131,116	38,853		
1890	1,444,933	47,638		
1900	1,883,669	69,844		
1910	2,537,167	89,760		
1920	3,155,900	117,132		
1930	4,041,334	208,828		
1940	4,160,165	226,973		
1950	4,835,329	318,565		
1960	6,066,782	514,875		
1970	7,168,164	770,292		
1980	7,364,823	925,066		

*Negligible

APPENDIXES

APPENDIX 3

BLACK POPULATION BY COUNTY—1790–1870

	TOTAL POPULATION	BLACKS Total	Free	Slave	BLACK PERCENTAGE OF TOTAL
1790					
Northern counties					
Bergen	12,601	2,493	192	2,301	19.8
Essex	17,785	1,331	160	1,171	7.5
Hunterdon	20,253	1,492	191	1,301	7.4
Middlesex	15,956	1,458	140	1,318	9.1
Monmouth	16,918	1,949	353	1,596	11.5
Morris	16,216	684	48	636	4.2
Somerset	12,296	1,957	147	1,810	15.9
Sussex	19,500	504	65	439	2.6
Total	131,525	11,868	1,296	10,572	9.0
Southern counties					
Burlington	18,095	825	598	227	4.6
Cape May	2,571	155	14	141	6.0
Cumberland	8,248	258	138	120	3.1
Gloucester	13,363	533	342	191	4.0
Salem	10,437	546	374	172	5.2
Total	52,714	2,317	1,466	851	4.4
1800					
Northern counties					
Bergen	15,156	3,027	202	2,825	20.0
Essex	22,269	1,719	198	1,521	7.7
Hudson	21,261	1,740	520	1,220	8.2
Middlesex	17,890	1,827	263	1,564	10.2
Monmouth	19,872	2,101	468	1,633	10.6
Morris	17,750	875	100	775	4.9
Somerset	12,815	2,038	175	1,863	15.9
Sussex	22,534	616	102	514	2.7
Total	149,547	13,943	2,028	11,915	9.3

Continued on next page

APPENDIXES

	TOTAL POPULATION	BLACKS Total	BLACKS Free	BLACKS Slave	BLACK PERCENTAGE OF TOTAL
Southern counties					
Burlington	21,521	958	770	188	4.5
Cape May	3,066	178	80	98	5.8
Cumberland	9,529	346	271	75	3.6
Gloucester	16,115	707	646	61	4.4
Salem	11,371	692	607	85	6.1
Total	61,602	2,881	2,374	507	4.7
1810					
Northern counties					
Bergen	16,603	2,965	785	2,180	17.9
Essex	25,984	1,887	758	1,129	7.3
Hunterdon	24,556	1,806	687	1,119	7.4
Middlesex	20,381	1,963	665	1,298	9.6
Monmouth	22,150	2,136	632	1,504	9.6
Morris	21,828	1,060	204	856	4.9
Somerset	14,725	2,284	316	1,968	15.5
Sussex	25,549	747	269	478	2.9
Total	171,776	14,848	4,316	10,532	8.6
Southern counties					
Burlington	24,972	1,039	946	93	4.2
Cape May	3,632	192	111	81	5.3
Cumberland	12,670	598	547	42	4.7
Gloucester	19,744	960	886	74	4.9
Salem	12,761	1,066	1,037	29	8.4
Total	73,779	3,855	3,527	319	5.2

Continued on next page

APPENDIXES

	TOTAL POPULATION	BLACKS Total	Free	Slave	BLACK PERCENTAGE OF TOTAL
1820					
Northern counties					
Bergen	18,178	2,742	1,059	1,683	15.1
Essex	30,793	2,049	1,390	659	6.7
Hunterdon	28,604	2,059	1,443	616	7.2
Middlesex	21,470	2,045	1,033	1,012	9.5
Monmouth	25,038	2,230	982	1,248	8.9
Morris	21,368	1,114	457	657	5.2
Somerset	16,506	2,609	1,487	1,122	15.8
Sussex	32,752	851	473	378	2.6
Total	194,709	15,699	8,324	7,375	8.1
Southern counties					
Burlington	28,822	1,343	1,261	82	4.7
Cape May	4,265	233	205	28	5.5
Cumberland	12,668	623	605	18	4.9
Gloucester	23,089	1,103	1,064	39	4.8
Salem	14,022	1,016	1,001	15	7.2
Total	82,866	4,318	4,136	182	5.2
1830					
Northern counties					
Bergen	22,412	2,478	1,894	584	11.1
Essex	41,911	2,157	1,939	218	5.2
Hunterdon	31,060	1,942	1,770	172	6.3
Middlesex	23,157	2,127	1,818	309	9.2
Monmouth	29,233	2,299	2,072	227	7.9
Morris	23,666	967	802	165	4.1
Somerset	17,689	2,307	1,859	448	13.0
Sussex	20,346	452	401	51	2.2
Warren	18,627	469	422	47	2.5
Total	228,101	15,198	12,977	2,221	6.7

Continued on next page

APPENDIXES

	TOTAL POPULATION	BLACKS Total	Free	Slave	BLACK PERCENTAGE OF TOTAL
Southern counties					
Burlington	31,107	1,378	1,355	23	4.4
Cape May	4,936	228	225	3	4.6
Cumberland	14,093	788	786	2	5.6
Gloucester	28,431	1,553	1,549	4	5.5
Salem	14,155	1,412	1,411	1	10.0
Total	92,722	5,359	5,326	33	5.8
1840					
Northern counties					
Bergen	13,223	1,751	1,529	222	13.2
Essex	44,621	1,928	1,908	20	4.3
Hudson	9,483	330	319	11	3.5
Hunterdon	24,789	813	778	35	3.3
Mercer	21,502	2,341	2,319	22	10.9
Middlesex	21,893	1,563	1,535	28	7.1
Monmouth	32,909	2,265	2,180	85	6.9
Morris	25,844	948	911	37	3.7
Passaic	16,734	792	706	86	4.7
Somerset	17,455	1,757	1,652	105	10.1
Sussex	21,770	367	354	13	1.7
Warren	20,366	463	455	8	2.3
Total	270,589	15,318	14,646	672	5.7
Southern counties					
Atlantic	8,726	234	234		2.7
Burlington	32,831	1,644	1,643	1	5.0
Cape May	5,324	198	198		3.7
Cumberland	14,374	896	896		6.2
Gloucester	25,438	1,631	1,631		6.4
Salem	16,024	1,797	1,796	1	11.2
Total	102,717	6,400	6,398	2	6.2

Continued on next page

APPENDIXES

	TOTAL POPULATION	BLACKS Total	Free	Slave	BLACK PERCENTAGE OF TOTAL
1850					
Northern counties					
Bergen	14,725	1,665	1,624	41	11.3
Essex	73,950	2,334	2,328	6	3.2
Hudson	21,822	503	500	3	2.3
Hunterdon	28,990	817	808	9	2.8
Mercer	27,992	2,042	2,036	6	7.3
Middlesex	28,635	1,380	1,369	11	4.8
Monmouth	30,313	2,398	2,323	75	7.9
Morris	30,158	1,027	1,008	19	3.4
Passaic	22,569	646	615	31	2.9
Somerset	19,692	1,742	1,711	31	8.8
Sussex	22,989	341	340	1	1.5
Warren	22,358	382	380	2	1.7
Total	344,193	15,277	15,042	235	4.4
Southern counties					
Atlantic	8,960	218	217	1	2.4
Burlington	43,203	2,109	2,109		4.9
Camden	25,422	2,230	2,230		8.8
Cape May	6,433	247	247		3.8
Cumberland	17,189	1,130	1,130		6.6
Gloucester	14,655	620	620		4.2
Ocean	10,032	140	140		1.4
Salem	19,467	2,075	2,075		10.7
Total	145,361	8,769	8,768	1	6.0

Continued on next page

APPENDIXES

	TOTAL POPULATION	BLACKS Total	Free	Slave	BLACK PERCENTAGE OF TOTAL
1860					
Northern counties					
Bergen	21,618	1,663	1,663		7.7
Essex	98,877	1,757	1,757		1.8
Hudson	62,717	653	653		1.0
Hunterdon	33,654	800	796	4	2.4
Mercer	37,419	2,225	2,225		6.0
Middlesex	34,812	1,308	1,307	1	3.8
Monmouth	39,346	2,658	2,658		6.8
Morris	34,677	687	686	1	2.0
Passaic	29,013	559	557	2	1.9
Somerset	22,057	1,597	1,588	9	7.2
Sussex	23,846	324	324		1.4
Union	27,780	865	864	1	3.1
Warren	28,433	387	387		1.4
Total	494,249	15,483	15,465	18	3.1
Southern counties					
Atlantic	11,786	194	194		1.6
Burlington	49,730	2,224	2,224		4.5
Camden	34,457	2,574	2,574		7.5
Cape May	7,130	273	273		3.8
Cumberland	22,605	1,295	1,295		5.7
Gloucester	18,444	707	707		3.8
Ocean	11,176	124	124		1.1
Salem	22,458	2,462	2,462		11.0
Total	177,786	9,853	9,853		5.5

Continued on next page

APPENDIXES

	TOTAL POPULATION	BLACKS Total	Free	Slave	BLACK PERCENTAGE OF TOTAL
1870					
Northern counties					
Bergen	30,122	1,632	1,632		5.4
Essex	143,839	2,539	2,539		1.8
Hudson	129,067	1,050	1,050		0.8
Hunterdon	36,963	634	634		1.7
Mercer	46,386	2,368	2,368		5.1
Middlesex	45,029	1,545	1,545		3.4
Monmouth	46,195	2,910	2,910		6.3
Morris	43,137	733	733		1.7
Passaic	46,416	675	675		1.5
Somerset	23,510	1,524	1,524		6.5
Sussex	23,168	196	196		0.9
Union	41,859	1,296	1,296		3.1
Warren	34,336	381	381		1.1
Total	690,027	17,483	17,483		2.5
Southern counties					
Atlantic	14,093	184	184		1.3
Burlington	53,639	2,540	2,540		4.7
Camden	46,193	4,430	4,430		9.6
Cape May	8,349	427	427		5.1
Cumberland	34,665	1,767	1,767		5.1
Gloucester	21,562	973	973		4.5
Ocean	13,628	117	117		0.9
Salem	23,940	2,737	2,737		11.4
Total	216,069	13,175	13,175		6.1

APPENDIX 4

BLACK POPULATION BY COUNTY—1880–1980

	TOTAL POPULATION	BLACK TOTAL	BLACK PERCENTAGE OF TOTAL
1880			
Northern counties			
Bergen	36,786	1,891	5.1
Essex	189,929	4,727	2.5
Hudson	187,944	1,655	0.9
Hunterdon	38,570	552	1.4
Mercer	58,061	3,230	5.6
Middlesex	52,286	1,625	3.1
Monmouth	55,538	3,461	6.2
Morris	50,861	810	1.6
Passaic	68,860	1,077	1.6
Somerset	27,162	1,659	6.1
Sussex	23,539	174	0.7
Union	55,571	1,939	3.5
Warren	36,589	356	1.0
Total	881,696	23,156	2.6
Southern counties			
Atlantic	18,704	894	4.8
Burlington	55,402	2,570	4.6
Camden	62,942	5,687	9.0
Cape May	9,765	570	5.8
Cumberland	37,687	1,965	5.2
Gloucester	25,886	1,144	4.4
Ocean	14,455	98	0.7
Salem	24,579	2,769	11.3
Total	249,420	15,697	6.3

Continued on next page

APPENDIXES

	TOTAL POPULATION	BLACK TOTAL	BLACK PERCENTAGE OF TOTAL
1890			
Northern counties			
Bergen	47,226	1,814	3.8
Essex	256,098	6,910	2.7
Hudson	275,126	2,456	0.9
Hunterdon	35,355	497	1.4
Mercer	79,978	3,467	4.3
Middlesex	61,754	1,643	2.7
Monmouth	69,128	5,074	7.3
Morris	54,101	956	1.8
Passaic	105,046	1,125	1.1
Somerset	28,311	1,348	9.9
Sussex	22,259	134	0.6
Union	72,467	2,202	3.0
Warren	36,553	305	0.8
Total	1,143,402	29,393	2.6
Southern counties			
Atlantic	28,836	2,267	7.9
Burlington	58,528	2,624	4.5
Camden	87,687	7,475	8.5
Cape May	11,268	861	7.6
Cumberland	45,438	2,100	4.6
Gloucester	28,649	1,417	4.9
Ocean	15,974	153	1.0
Salem	25,150	2,810	5.4
Total	301,531	18,245	6.1

Continued on next page

	TOTAL POPULATION	BLACK TOTAL	BLACK PERCENTAGE OF TOTAL
1900			
Northern counties			
Bergen	78,441	2,600	3.3
Essex	359,053	12,559	3.5
Hudson	386,048	4,439	1.1
Hunterdon	34,507	518	1.5
Mercer	95,365	4,152	4.4
Middlesex	79,762	1,900	2.4
Monmouth	82,057	6,907	8.4
Morris	65,156	1,618	2.5
Passaic	155,202	1,949	1.3
Somerset	32,948	1,559	4.7
Sussex	24,134	160	0.7
Union	99,353	3,854	3.9
Warren	37,781	367	1.0
Total	1,529,807	42,582	2.8
Southern counties			
Atlantic	46,402	6,920	14.9
Burlington	58,241	3,130	5.4
Camden	107,643	8,583	8.0
Cape May	13,201	869	6.6
Cumberland	51,193	2,403	4.7
Gloucester	31,905	2,058	6.5
Ocean	19,747	270	1.4
Salem	25,530	3,029	11.9
Total	353,862	27,262	7.7

Continued on next page

APPENDIXES

	TOTAL POPULATION	BLACK TOTAL	BLACK PERCENTAGE OF TOTAL
1910			
Northern counties			
Bergen	138,002	3,295	2.4
Essex	512,886	18,104	3.5
Hudson	537,231	7,173	1.3
Hunterdon	33,569	438	1.3
Mercer	125,657	5,125	4.1
Middlesex	114,426	1,846	1.6
Monmouth	94,734	8,279	8.7
Morris	74,704	1,940	2.6
Passaic	215,902	2,401	1.1
Somerset	38,820	1,414	3.6
Sussex	26,781	168	0.6
Union	140,197	5,353	3.8
Warren	43,187	364	0.8
Total	2,096,096	55,900	2.7
Southern counties			
Atlantic	71,894	10,782	15.0
Burlington	66,565	3,454	5.2
Camden	142,029	9,402	6.6
Cape May	19,745	1,444	7.3
Cumberland	55,153	2,641	4.8
Gloucester	37,368	2,375	6.4
Ocean	21,318	438	2.1
Salem	26,999	3,324	12.3
Total	441,071	33,860	7.7

Continued on next page

APPENDIXES

	TOTAL POPULATION	BLACK TOTAL	BLACK PERCENTAGE OF TOTAL
1920			
Northern counties			
Bergen	210,703	4,136	2.0
Essex	652,089	28,956	4.4
Hudson	629,154	9,351	1.5
Hunterdon	32,885	359	1.1
Mercer	159,881	6,991	4.4
Middlesex	162,334	2,815	1.7
Monmouth	104,925	8,938	8.5
Morris	82,694	1,861	2.3
Passaic	259,174	2,522	1.0
Somerset	47,991	1,221	2.5
Sussex	24,905	90	0.4
Union	200,157	8,087	4.0
Warren	45,057	272	0.6
Total	2,611,949	75,599	2.9
Southern counties			
Atlantic	83,914	12,597	15.0
Burlington	81,770	4,493	5.5
Camden	190,508	12,107	6.4
Cape May	19,460	1,560	8.0
Cumberland	61,348	3,094	5.0
Gloucester	48,224	3,154	6.5
Ocean	22,155	566	2.6
Salem	36,572	3,962	10.8
Total	543,951	41,533	7.6

Continued on next page

APPENDIXES

	TOTAL POPULATION	BLACK TOTAL	BLACK PERCENTAGE OF TOTAL
1930			
Northern counties			
Bergen	364,977	8,872	2.4
Essex	833,513	60,236	7.2
Hudson	690,730	15,970	2.3
Hunterdon	34,728	407	1.2
Mercer	187,143	11,949	6.4
Middlesex	212,208	5,895	2.8
Monmouth	147,209	13,897	9.4
Morris	110,445	3,269	3.0
Passaic	302,129	5,518	1.8
Somerset	65,132	1,628	2.5
Sussex	27,830	119	0.4
Union	305,209	17,859	5.9
Warren	49,319	303	0.6
Total	3,330,572	145,922	4.4
Southern counties			
Atlantic	124,823	19,703	15.8
Burlington	93,541	6,762	7.2
Camden	252,312	16,813	6.7
Cape May	29,486	2,782	9.4
Cumberland	69,895	4,748	6.8
Gloucester	70,802	6,077	8.6
Ocean	33,069	1,258	3.8
Salem	36,834	4,763	12.9
Total	710,762	62,906	8.9

Continued on next page

APPENDIXES

	TOTAL POPULATION	BLACK TOTAL	BLACK PERCENTAGE OF TOTAL
1940			
Northern counties			
Bergen	409,646	9,733	2.4
Essex	837,340	68,776	8.2
Hudson	652,040	16,147	2.5
Hunterdon	36,766	586	1.6
Mercer	197,318	13,876	7.0
Middlesex	217,077	5,788	2.7
Monmouth	161,238	14,162	8.8
Morris	125,732	3,203	2.6
Passaic	309,353	6,776	2.2
Somerset	74,390	1,823	2.5
Sussex	29,632	121	0.4
Union	328,344	19,699	6.0
Warren	50,181	350	0.7
Total	3,429,057	161,040	4.7
Southern counties			
Atlantic	124,066	19,892	16.0
Burlington	97,013	6,987	7.2
Camden	255,727	17,933	7.0
Cape May	28,919	2,618	9.1
Cumberland	73,184	5,388	7.4
Gloucester	72,219	6,767	9.4
Ocean	37,706	1,330	3.5
Salem	42,274	5,018	11.9
Total	731,108	65,933	9.0

Continued on next page

APPENDIXES

	TOTAL POPULATION	BLACK TOTAL	BLACK PERCENTAGE OF TOTAL
1950			
Northern counties			
Bergen	539,139	10,899	2.0
Essex	905,949	104,307	11.5
Hudson	647,437	23,780	3.7
Hunterdon	42,736	883	2.1
Mercer	229,781	20,427	8.9
Middlesex	264,872	9,685	3.7
Monmouth	225,327	20,415	9.1
Morris	164,371	4,108	2.5
Passaic	337,093	11,991	3.6
Somerset	99,052	3,111	3.1
Sussex	34,423	116	0.3
Union	398,138	25,316	6.4
Warren	54,374	325	0.6
Total	3,942,692	235,363	6.0
Southern counties			
Atlantic	132,399	21,506	16.2
Burlington	135,910	10,926	8.0
Camden	300,743	22,625	7.5
Cape May	37,131	2,895	7.8
Cumberland	88,597	8,826	10.0
Gloucester	91,727	8,684	9.5
Ocean	56,622	1,536	2.7
Salem	49,508	6,204	12.5
Total	892,637	83,202	9.3

Continued on next page

APPENDIXES

	TOTAL POPULATION	BLACK TOTAL	BLACK PERCENTAGE OF TOTAL
1960			
Northern counties			
Bergen	780,255	16,269	2.1
Essex	923,545	180,737	19.6
Hudson	610,734	41,327	6.8
Hunterdon	54,107	1,128	2.1
Mercer	266,392	33,714	12.7
Middlesex	433,856	16,489	3.8
Monmouth	334,401	30,730	9.2
Morris	261,620	5,375	2.1
Passaic	406,618	26,799	6.6
Somerset	143,913	4,476	3.1
Sussex	49,255	160	0.3
Union	504,255	37,972	7.5
Warren	63,220	542	0.9
Total	4,832,171	395,718	8.2
Southern counties			
Atlantic	160,880	28,225	17.5
Burlington	224,499	14,280	6.4
Camden	392,035	35,297	9.0
Cape May	48,555	3,902	8.0
Cumberland	106,850	13,028	12.2
Gloucester	134,840	12,262	9.1
Ocean	108,241	3,351	3.1
Salem	58,711	8,812	15.0
Total	1,234,611	119,157	9.7

Continued on next page

APPENDIXES

	TOTAL POPULATION	BLACK TOTAL	BLACK PERCENTAGE OF TOTAL
1970			
Northern counties			
Bergen	898,012	24,915	2.8
Essex	929,986	279,136	30.0
Hudson	609,266	61,095	10.0
Hunterdon	69,718	1,166	1.7
Mercer	303,968	49,802	16.4
Middlesex	583,813	26,067	4.5
Monmouth	459,379	38,275	8.3
Morris	383,454	8,483	2.2
Passaic	460,782	50,199	10.9
Somerset	198,372	7,166	3.6
Sussex	77,528	311	0.4
Union	543,116	60,723	11.2
Warren	73,879	795	1.1
Total	5,591,273	608,133	10.9
Southern counties			
Atlantic	175,043	30,403	17.4
Burlington	323,132	28,162	8.8
Camden	456,291	52,318	11.5
Cape May	59,554	4,772	8.0
Cumberland	121,374	16,566	13.7
Gloucester	172,681	14,444	8.4
Ocean	208,470	6,261	3.0
Salem	60,346	9,233	15.3
Total	1,576,891	162,159	10.3

Continued on next page

APPENDIXES

	TOTAL POPULATION	BLACK TOTAL	BLACK PERCENTAGE OF TOTAL
1980			
Northern counties			
Bergen	845,385	33,043	3.9
Essex	851,116	316,440	37.2
Hudson	556,972	70,050	12.6
Hunterdon	87,361	1,123	1.3
Mercer	307,863	55,545	18.0
Middlesex	595,893	35,768	6.0
Monmouth	503,173	42,985	8.5
Morris	407,630	10,017	2.5
Passaic	447,585	59,171	13.2
Somerset	203,129	10,123	5.0
Sussex	116,119	680	0.6
Union	504,094	81,207	16.1
Warren	84,429	933	1.1
Total	5,510,749	717,085	13.0
Southern counties			
Atlantic	194,119	34,134	17.6
Burlington	362,542	45,471	12.5
Camden	471,650	67,232	14.3
Cape May	82,266	5,157	6.3
Cumberland	132,866	19,868	15.0
Gloucester	199,917	16,936	8.5
Ocean	346,038	9,439	2.7
Salem	64,676	9,744	15.1
Total	1,854,074	207,981	11.2

Suggested Readings

Calligaro, Lee. "The Negro's Legal Status in Pre-Civil War New Jersey." *New Jersey History* 70 (1967).

Crew, Spencer R. "Making Their Own Way: Black Social and Institutional Life in Camden, New Jersey, 1860-1920." *The Black Experience in Southern New Jersey.* Camden County Historical Society. Camden, 1985.

Foster, Herbert J. "Institutional Development in the Black Community of Atlantic City, New Jersey: 1850-1930." *The Black Experience in Southern New Jersey.* Camden County Historical Society. Camden, 1985.

Gardner, D. H. "The Emancipation of Slaves in New Jersey." *Proceedings of the New Jersey Historical Society* 9 (1924).

Greene, Larry A. "The Emancipation Proclamation in New Jersey and the Paranoid Style." *New Jersey History* 91 (Summer 1973).

Hagan, Lee, Larry A. Greene, Leonard Harris, and Clement A. Price. "New Jersey Afro-Americans: From Colonial Times to the Present." *The New Jersey Ethnic Experience.* Edited by Barbara Cunningham. Union City, 1977.

Interracial Committee of the New Jersey Conference of Social Work. *The Negro in New Jersey.* Newark, 1932.

Lyght, Ernest. *Path of Freedom: The Black Presence in New Jersey's Burlington County, 1659-1900.* Cherry Hill, 1978.

MacManus, Edward. *Black Bondage in the North.* Syracuse, 1973.

Moss, Simeon F. "The Persistence of Slavery and Involuntary Servitude in a Free State (1685-1866)." *Journal of Negro History* 35 (1950).

Pingeon, Frances D. "Slavery in New Jersey on the Eve of Revolution." *New Jersey in the American Revolution: Political and Social Conflict.* Edited by William C. Wright. Trenton, 1974.

──────. "Dissenting Attitudes Toward the Negro in New Jersey—1837." *New Jersey History* 89 (1971).

SUGGESTED READINGS

Price, Clement Alexander. Freedom Not Far Distant: *A Documentary History of Afro-Americans in New Jersey.* Newark, 1980.

⸻ . "The Strange Career of Race Relations in New Jersey History." *The Black Experience in Southern New Jersey.* Camden County Historical Society. Camden, 1985.

⸻ . "We Knew Our Place, We Knew Our Way: Lessons From the Black Past of Southern New Jersey." *Blacks in New Jersey, 1986 Report. A Review of Blacks in South Jersey.* New Jersey Public Policy Research Institute.

Wacker, Peter O. "Patterns and Problems in the Historical Geography of the Afro-American Population of New Jersey, 1726–1860." *Pattern and Process: Research in Historical Geography.* Edited by Ralph Ehrenberg. Washington, D.C., 1975.

Wright, Marion M. Thompson. *The Education of Negroes in New Jersey.* New York, 1941.

⸻ ."New Jersey Laws and the Negro." *Journal of Negro History* 28 (1943).

⸻ . "Negro Suffrage in New Jersey, 1776–1875." *Journal of Negro History* 33 (1948).

Zilversmit, Arthur. The First Emancipation: *The Abolition of Slavery in the North. Chicago, 1967.*